莎士比亚四大喜剧
英汉对照

Twelfth Night

第 十 二 夜

【英】莎士比亚 著　朱生豪 译

燕山大学出版社
YANSHAN UNIVERSITY PRESS
2018·秦皇岛

图书在版编目（CIP）数据

第十二夜：英汉对照/（英）莎士比亚著；朱生豪译 .—秦皇岛：燕山大学出版社，2018.3（2022.3 重印）

（莎士比亚四大喜剧）

ISBN 978-7-81142-596-3

Ⅰ . ①第… Ⅱ . ①莎…②朱… Ⅲ . ①英语—汉语—对照读物②悲剧—剧本—英国—中世纪 Ⅳ . ① H319.4：I

中国版本图书馆 CIP 数据核字（2022）第 033044 号

第十二夜：英汉对照

（英）莎士比亚著；朱生豪译 .

出 版 人：陈 玉		
责任编辑：唐 雷	丛书策划：陈 玉 陈亚明	
封面设计：金 帆	责任印制：吴 波	
出版发行：燕山大学出版社	地 址：河北省秦皇岛市河北大街西段 438 号	
邮政编码：066004	电 话：0335-8387555	
印 刷：天津盛奥传媒印务有限公司	经 销：全国新华书店	
尺 寸：170mm×240mm 1/16	印 张：13	字 数：180 千字
版 次：2018 年 3 月第 1 版	印 次：2022 年 3 月第 3 次印刷	
书 号：ISBN 978-7-81142-596-3		
定 价：45.00 元		

版权所有 侵权必究

如发生印刷、装订质量问题，读者可与出版社联系调换

联系电话：0335-8387718

剧中人物

DUKE 奥西诺：伊利里亚公爵

SEBASTIAN 西巴斯辛：薇奥拉之兄

ANTONIO 安东尼奥：船长，西巴斯辛之友

CAPTAIN 船长：薇奥拉之友

VALENTINE 凡伦丁：公爵侍臣

CURIO 丘里奥：公爵侍臣

SIR TOBY 托比·培尔契爵士：奥丽维娅的叔父

SIR ANDREW AGUECHEEK 安德鲁·艾古契克爵士

MALVOLIO 马伏里奥：奥丽维娅的管家

FABIAN 费边：小丑 奥丽维娅之仆

OLIVIA 奥丽维娅：富有的伯爵小姐

VIOLA 薇奥拉：热恋公爵者

MARIA 玛利娅：奥丽维娅的侍女

CLOWN 小丑

群臣、牧师、水手、警吏、乐工及其他侍从等

 # 地点

伊利里亚某城及其附近海滨。

Contents 目录

ACT I　第一幕

SCENE Ⅰ ｜ 第一场 ·················2
SCENE Ⅱ ｜ 第二场 ·················6
SCENE Ⅲ ｜ 第三场 ················12
SCENE Ⅳ ｜ 第四场 ················22
SCENE Ⅴ ｜ 第五场 ················26

ACT Ⅱ　第二幕

SCENE Ⅰ ｜ 第一场 ················50
SCENE Ⅱ ｜ 第二场 ················54
SCENE Ⅲ ｜ 第三场 ················58
SCENE Ⅳ ｜ 第四场 ················70
SCENE Ⅴ ｜ 第五场 ················80

ACT Ⅲ　第三幕

SCENE Ⅰ ｜ 第一场 ················96
SCENE Ⅱ ｜ 第二场 ···············108
SCENE Ⅲ ｜ 第三场 ···············114
SCENE Ⅳ ｜ 第四场 ···············118

ACT Ⅳ　第四幕

SCENE Ⅰ ｜ 第一场 ···············148
SCENE Ⅱ ｜ 第二场 ···············154

SCENE Ⅲ ｜第三场 ·· 164

ACT V　第五幕
SCENE Ⅰ ｜第一场 ·· 170

ACT I 第一幕

SCENE I

A room in DUKE ORSINO's palace.
Enter DUKE ORSINO, CURIO, and other Lords; Musicians attending.

DUKE   If music be the food of love, play on;
Give me excess of it, that, surfeiting,
The appetite may sicken, and so die.
That strain again! it had a dying fall:
O, it came o'er my ear like the sweet sound,
That breathes upon a bank of violets,
Stealing and giving odour! Enough; no more:
'Tis not so sweet now as it was before.
O spirit of love! how quick and fresh art thou,
That, notwithstanding thy capacity
Receiveth as the sea, nought enters there,
Of what validity and pitch soe'er,
But falls into abatement and low price,
Even in a minute: so full of shapes is fancy
That it alone is high fantastical.

CURIO   Will you go hunt, my lord?

DUKE   What, Curio?

CURIO   The hart.

DUKE   Why, so I do, the noblest that I have:
O, when mine eyes did see Olivia first,
Methought she purged the air of pestilence!
That instant was I turn'd into a hart;
And my desires, like fell and cruel hounds,
E'er since pursue me.

Enter VALENTINE.

DUKE   How now! what news from her?

第一场

公爵府中一室。

公爵、丘里奥、众臣同上；乐工随侍。

公　　爵　假如音乐是爱情的食粮，那么奏下去吧；尽量地奏下去，好让爱情因过饱噎塞而死。又奏起这个调子来了！它有一种渐渐消沉下去的节奏。啊！它经过我的耳畔，就像微风吹拂一丛紫罗兰，发出轻柔的声音，一面把花香偷走，一面又把花香分送。够了！别再奏下去了！它现在已经不像原来那样甜蜜了。爱情的精灵呀！你是多么敏感而活泼；虽然你有海一样的容量，可是无论怎样高贵超越的事物，一进了你的范围，便会在顷刻间失去了它的价值。爱情是这样充满了意象，在一切事物中是最富于幻想的。

丘 里 奥　殿下，您要不要去打猎？
公　　爵　什么，丘里奥？
丘 里 奥　去打鹿。
公　　爵　啊，一点不错，我的心就像是一头鹿。唉！当我第一眼瞧见奥丽维娅的时候，我觉得好像空气给她澄清了。那时我就变成了一头鹿；从此我的情欲像凶暴残酷的猎犬一样，永远追逐着我。

凡伦丁上。

公　　爵　怎样！她那边有什么消息？

VALENTINE So please my lord, I might not be admitted;
But from her handmaid do return this answer:
The element itself, till seven years' heat,
Shall not behold her face at ample view;
But, like a cloistress, she will veiled walk
And water once a day her chamber round
With eye-offending brine: all this to season
A brother's dead love, which she would keep fresh
And lasting in her sad remembrance.

DUKE O, she that hath a heart of that fine frame
To pay this debt of love but to a brother,
How will she love, when the rich golden shaft
Hath kill'd the flock of all affections else
That live in her; when liver, brain and heart,
These sovereign thrones, are all supplied, and fill'd
Her sweet perfections with one self king!
Away before me to sweet beds of flowers:
Love-thoughts lie rich when canopied with bowers.

Exeunt.

凡伦丁　启禀殿下，他们不让我进去，只从她的侍女嘴里传来了这一个答复：除非再过七个寒暑，就是青天也不能窥见她的全貌；她要像一个尼姑一样，蒙着面幕而行，每天用辛酸的眼泪浇洒她的卧室：这一切都是为着纪念对于一个死去的哥哥的爱，她要把对哥哥的爱永远活生生地保留在她悲伤的记忆里。

公　爵　唉！她有这么一颗优美的心，对于她的哥哥也会挚爱到这等地步。假如爱神那枝有力的金箭把她心里一切其他的感情一齐射死；假如只有一个唯一的君王占据着她的心肝头脑——这些尊严的御座，这些珍美的财宝——那时她将要怎样恋爱着啊！给我引道到芬芳的花丛；相思在花荫下格外情浓。

同下。

SCENE II

The sea-coast.
Enter VIOLA, a Captain, and Sailors.

VIOLA What country, friends, is this?
Captain This is Illyria, lady.
VIOLA And what should I do in Illyria?
My brother he is in Elysium.
Perchance he is not drown'd: what think you, sailors?
Captain It is perchance that you yourself were saved.
VIOLA O my poor brother! and so perchance may he be.
Captain True, madam: and, to comfort you with chance,
Assure yourself, after our ship did split,
When you and those poor number saved with you
Hung on our driving boat, I saw your brother,
Most provident in peril, bind himself,
Courage and hope both teaching him the practise,
To a strong mast that lived upon the sea;
Where, like Arion on the dolphin's back,
I saw him hold acquaintance with the waves
So long as I could see.
VIOLA For saying so, there's gold:
Mine own escape unfoldeth to my hope,
Whereto thy speech serves for authority,
The like of him. Know'st thou this country?
Captain Ay, madam, well; for I was bred and born
Not three hours' travel from this very place.
VIOLA Who governs here?
Captain A noble duke, in nature as in name.

第二场

海滨。
薇奥拉、船长及水手等上。

薇 奥 拉　朋友们,这儿是什么国土?
船　　长　这儿是伊利里亚,姑娘。
薇 奥 拉　我在伊利里亚干什么呢?我的哥哥已经到极乐世界里去了。也许他侥幸没有淹死。水手们,你们以为怎样?
船　　长　您也是侥幸才保全了性命的。
薇 奥 拉　唉,我的可怜的哥哥!但愿他也侥幸无恙!
船　　长　不错,姑娘,您可以用侥幸的希望来宽慰您自己。我告诉您,我们的船撞破了之后,您和那几个跟您一同脱险的人紧攀着我们那只给风涛所颠摇的小船,那时我瞧见您的哥哥很有急智地把他自己捆在一根浮在海面的桅墙上,勇敢和希望教给了他这个计策;我见他像阿里翁①骑在海豚背上似的浮沉在波浪之间,直到我的眼睛望不见他。
薇 奥 拉　你的话使我很高兴,请收下这点钱,聊表谢意。由于我自己脱险,使我抱着他也能够同样脱险的希望;你的话更把我的希望证实了几分。你知道这国土吗?
船　　长　是的,姑娘,很熟悉;因为我就是在离这儿不到三小时旅程的地方生长的。
薇 奥 拉　谁统治着这地方?
船　　长　一位名实相符的高贵的公爵。

---

① 阿里翁(Arion),希腊诗人和音乐家,传说他在某次乘船自西西里至科林多,途中为水手所迫害,"因跃入海中",为海豚负至岸上,盖深感其音乐之力云。

VIOLA	What is the name?
Captain	Orsino.
VIOLA	Orsino! I have heard my father name him:
	He was a bachelor then.
Captain	And so is now, or was so very late;
	For but a month ago I went from hence,
	And then 'twas fresh in murmur,—as, you know,
	What great ones do the less will prattle of,—
	That he did seek the love of fair Olivia.
VIOLA	What's she?
Captain	A virtuous maid, the daughter of a count
	That died some twelvemonth since, then leaving her
	In the protection of his son, her brother,
	Who shortly also died: for whose dear love,
	They say, she hath abjured the company
	And sight of men.
VIOLA	O that I served that lady
	And might not be delivered to the world,
	Till I had made mine own occasion mellow,
	What my estate is!
Captain	That were hard to compass;
	Because she will admit no kind of suit,
	No, not the duke's.
VIOLA	There is a fair behavior in thee, captain;
	And though that nature with a beauteous wall
	Doth oft close in pollution, yet of thee
	I will believe thou hast a mind that suits
	With this thy fair and outward character.
	I prithee, and I'll pay thee bounteously,
	Conceal me what I am, and be my aid
	For such disguise as haply shall become

薇奥拉	他叫什么名字？
船　长	奥西诺。
薇奥拉	奥西诺！我曾经听见我父亲说起过他；那时他还没有娶亲。
船　长	现在他还是这样，至少在最近我还不曾听见他娶亲的消息；因为只一个月之前我从这儿出发，那时刚刚有一种新鲜的风传——您知道大人物的一举一动，都会被一般人纷纷议论着的——说他在向美貌的奥丽维娅求爱。
薇奥拉	她是谁呀？
船　长	她是一位品德高尚的姑娘；她的父亲是位伯爵，约莫在一年前死去，把她交给他的儿子，她的哥哥照顾，可是他不久又死了。他们说为了对于她哥哥的深切的友爱，她已经发誓不再跟男人们在一起或是见他们的面。
薇奥拉	唉！要是我能够侍候这位小姐，就可以不用在时机没有成熟之前泄露我的身份了。
船　长	那很难办到，因为她不肯接纳无论哪一种请求，就是公爵的请求她也是拒绝的。
薇奥拉	船长，你瞧上去是个好人；虽然造物常常用一层美丽的墙来围蔽住内中的污秽，但是我可以相信你的心地跟你的外表一样好。请你替我保守秘密，不要把我的真相泄露出去，我以后会重谢你的；你得帮助我假扮起来，好让我达到我的目的。我要去侍候这位公爵，你可以把我送给他作为一个净了身的传童；也许你会得到些好处的，因为我会唱歌，用各种的音乐向他说话，使他重用我。 以后有什么事以后再说；我会使计谋，你只需静默。

	The form of my intent. I'll serve this duke:
	Thou shall present me as an eunuch to him:
	It may be worth thy pains; for I can sing
	And speak to him in many sorts of music
	That will allow me very worth his service.
	What else may hap to time I will commit;
	Only shape thou thy silence to my wit.
Captain	Be you his eunuch, and your mute I'll be:
	When my tongue blabs, then let mine eyes not see.
VIOLA	I thank thee: lead me on.

Exeunt.

船　　长　　我便当哑巴，你去做近侍；
　　　　　　倘多话挖去我的眼珠子。
薇 奥 拉　　谢谢你；领着我去吧。

　　　　　　　　　　同下。

SCENE III

OLIVIA'S house.
Enter SIR TOBY BELCH and MARIA.

SIR TOBY   What a plague means my niece, to take the death of her brother thus? I am sure care's an enemy to life.

MARIA   By my troth, Sir Toby, you must come in earlier o' nights: your cousin, my lady, takes great exceptions to your ill hours.

SIR TOBY   Why, let her except, before excepted.

MARIA   Ay, but you must confine yourself within the modest limits of order.

SIR TOBY   Confine! I'll confine myself no finer than I am: these clothes are good enough to drink in; and so be hese boots too: an they be not, let them hang themselves in their own straps.

MARIA   That quaffing and drinking will undo you: I heard my lady talk of it yesterday; and of a foolish knight that you brought in one night here to be her wooer.

SIR TOBY   Who, Sir Andrew Aguecheek?

MARIA   Ay, he.

SIR TOBY   He's as tall a man as any's in Illyria.

MARIA   What's that to the purpose?

SIR TOBY   Why, he has three thousand ducats a year.

MARIA   Ay, but he'll have but a year in all these ducats: he's a very fool and a prodigal.

SIR TOBY   Fie, that you'll say so! he plays o' the viol-de-gamboys, and speaks three or four languages word for word without book, and hath all the good gifts of nature.

MARIA   He hath indeed, almost natural: for besides that he's a fool, he's a great quarreller: and but that he hath the gift of a coward to allay the gust he hath in quarrelling, 'tis thought among the prudent he would quickly have the gift of a grave.

第三场

奥丽维娅宅中一室。
托比·培尔契爵士及玛利娅上。

托　　比　　我的侄女见什么鬼把她哥哥的死看得那么重？悲哀是要损寿的呢。

玛利娅　　真的，托比老爷，您晚上得早点儿回来；您那侄小姐很反对您深夜不归呢。

托　　比　　哼，让她去今天反对、明天反对，尽管反对下去吧。

玛利娅　　哦，但是您总得有个分寸，不要太失身份才是。

托　　比　　身份！我这身衣服难道不合身份吗？穿了这种衣服去喝酒，也很有身份的了；还有这双靴子，要是它们不合身份，就叫它们在靴带上吊死了吧。

玛利娅　　您这样酗酒会作践了您自己的，我昨天听见小姐说起过；她还说起您有一晚带到这儿来向她求婚的那个傻骑士。

托　　比　　谁？安德鲁·艾古契克爵士吗？

玛利娅　　嗷，就是他。

托　　比　　他在伊利里亚也算是一表人才了。

玛利娅　　那又有什么相干？

托　　比　　哼，他一年有三千块钱收入呢。

玛利娅　　哦，可是一年之内就把这些钱全花光了。他是个大傻瓜，而且是个浪子。

托　　比　　呸！你说出这种话来！他会拉低音提琴；他会不看书本讲三四国文字，一个字都不模糊；他有很好的天分。

玛利娅　　是的，傻子都是得天独厚的；因为他除了是个傻瓜之外，又是一个惯会惹是招非的家伙；要是他没有懦夫的天分来缓和一下他那喜欢吵架的脾气，有见识的人都以为他就会有棺材睡的。

SIR TOBY By this hand, they are scoundrels and subtractors that say so of him. Who are they?

MARIA They that add, moreover, he's drunk nightly in your company.

SIR TOBY With drinking healths to my niece: I'll drink to her as long as there is a passage in my throat and drink in Illyria: He's a coward and a coystril that will not drink to my niece till his brains turn o' the toe like a parish-top. What, wench! Castiliano vulgo! for here comes Sir Andrew Aguecheek.

Enter SIR ANDREW.

SIR ANDREW Sir Toby Belch! how now, Sir Toby Belch!

SIR TOBY Sweet Sir Andrew!

SIR ANDREW Bless you, fair shrew.

MARIA And you too, sir.

SIR TOBY Accost, Sir Andrew, accost.

SIR ANDREW What's that?

SIR TOBY My niece's chambermaid.

SIR ANDREW Good Mistress Accost, I desire better acquaintance.

MARIA My name is Mary, sir.

SIR ANDREW Good Mistress Mary Accost,—

SIR TOBY You mistake, knight; 'accost' is front her, board her, woo her, assail her.

SIR ANDREW By my troth, I would not undertake her in this company. Is that the meaning of 'accost'?

MARIA Fare you well, gentlemen.

SIR TOBY An thou let part so, Sir Andrew, would thou mightst never draw sword again.

SIR ANDREW An you part so, mistress, I would I might never draw sword again. Fair lady, do you think you have fools in hand?

MARIA Sir, I have not you by the hand.

SIR ANDREW Marry, but you shall have; and here's my hand.

托　　比	我举手发誓，这样说他的人，都是一批坏蛋，信口雌黄的东西。他们是谁啊？
玛利娅	他们又说您每夜跟他在一块儿喝酒。
托　　比	我们都喝酒祝我的侄女健康呢。只要我的喉咙里有食道，伊利里亚有酒，我便要为她举杯祝饮。谁要是不愿为我的侄女举杯祝饮，喝到像拙陀螺似的天旋地转，他就是个不中用的汉子，是个卑鄙小人。嘿，丫头！放正经些！安德鲁·艾古契克爵士来啦。

　　　　　　　　　　安德鲁·艾古契克爵士上。

安德鲁	托比·培尔契爵士！您好，托比·培尔契爵士！
托　　比	亲爱的安德鲁爵士！
安德鲁	您好，美貌的小泼妇！
玛利娅	您好，大人。
托　　比	寒暄几句，安德鲁爵士，寒暄几句。
安德鲁	您说什么？
托　　比	这是舍侄女的丫环。
安德鲁	好寒萱姊姊，我希望咱们多多结识。
玛利娅	我的名字是玛丽，大人。
安德鲁	好玛丽·寒萱姊姊，——
托　　比	你弄错了，骑士；"寒暄几句"就是跑上去向她应酬一下，招呼一下，客套一下，来一下的意思。
安德鲁	哎哟，当着这些人我可不能跟她打交道。"寒暄"就是这个意思吗？
玛利娅	再见，先生们。
托　　比	要是你让她这样走了,安德鲁爵士,你以后再不用充汉子了。
安德鲁	要是你这样走了，姑娘，我以后再不用充汉子了。好小姐，你以为你手边是些傻瓜吗？
玛利娅	大人，可是我还不曾跟您握手呢。
安德鲁	那很好办，让我们握手。

MARIA Now, sir, 'thought is free:' I pray you, bring your hand to the buttery-bar and let it drink.

SIR ANDREW Wherefore, sweet-heart? what's your metaphor?

MARIA It's dry, sir.

SIR ANDREW Why, I think so: I am not such an ass but I can keep my hand dry. But what's your jest?

MARIA A dry jest, sir.

SIR ANDREW Are you full of them?

MARIA Ay, sir, I have them at my fingers' ends: marry, now I let go your hand, I am barren.

Exit.

SIR TOBY O knight thou lackest a cup of canary: when did I see thee so put down?

SIR ANDREW Never in your life, I think; unless you see canary put me down. Methinks sometimes I have no more wit than a Christian or an ordinary man has: but I am a great eater of beef and I believe that does harm to my wit.

SIR TOBY No question.

SIR ANDREW An I thought that, I'ld forswear it. I'll ride home to-morrow, Sir Toby.

SIR TOBY Pourquoi, my dear knight?

SIR ANDREW What is 'Pourquoi'? do or not do? I would I had bestowed that time in the tongues that I have in fencing, dancing and bear-baiting: O, had I but followed the arts!

SIR TOBY Then hadst thou had an excellent head of hair.

SIR ANDREW Why, would that have mended my hair?

SIR TOBY Past question; for thou seest it will not curl by nature.

SIR ANDREW But it becomes me well enough, does't not?

玛利娅　　好了，大人，思想是无拘无束的。请您把这只手带到卖酒的柜台那里去，让它喝两盅吧。

安德鲁　　这怎么讲，好人儿？你在打什么比方？

玛利娅　　我是说它怪没劲的。

安德鲁　　是啊，我也这样想。不管人家怎么说我蠢，应该好好保养两手的道理我还懂得。可是你说的是什么笑话？

玛利娅　　没劲的笑话。

安德鲁　　你一肚子都是这种笑话吗？

玛利娅　　不错，大人，满手里抓的也都是。得，现在我放开您的手了，我的笑料也都吹了。

下。

托　比　　骑士啊！你应该喝杯酒儿。几时我见你这样给人愚弄过？

安德鲁　　我想你从来没有见过；除非你见我被酒弄昏了头。有时我觉得我跟一般基督徒和平常人一样笨；可是我是个吃牛肉的老饕，我相信那对于我的聪明很有妨害。

托　比　　一定一定。

安德鲁　　要是我真那样想的话，以后我得戒了。托比爵士，明天我要骑马回家去了。

托　比　　Pourquoi①，我的亲爱的骑士？

安德鲁　　什么叫Pourquoi？好还是不好？我理该把我花在击剑、跳舞和耍熊上面的工夫学几种外国话的。唉！要是我读了文学多么好！

托　比　　要是你花些工夫在你的鬈发钳②上头，你就可以有一头很好的头发了。

安德鲁　　怎么，那跟我的头发有什么关系？

托　比　　很明白，因为你瞧你的头发不用些工夫上去是不会鬈曲起来的。

安德鲁　　可是我的头发不也已经够好看了吗？

---

① 法文"为什么"之意。
② 原文卷发钳(tongs)与外国话(tongues)音相近。

SIR TOBY Excellent; it hangs like flax on a distaff; and I hope to see a housewife take thee between her legs and spin it off.

SIR ANDREW Faith, I'll home to-morrow, Sir Toby: your niece will not be seen; or if she be, it's four to one she'll none of me: the count himself here hard by woos her.

SIR TOBY She'll none o' the count: she'll not match above her degree, neither in estate, years, nor wit; I have heard her swear't. Tut, there's life in't, man.

SIR ANDREW I'll stay a month longer. I am a fellow o' the strangest mind i' the world; I delight in masques and revels sometimes altogether.

SIR TOBY Art thou good at these kickchawses, knight?

SIR ANDREW As any man in Illyria, whatsoever he be, under the degree of my betters; and yet I will not compare with an old man.

SIR TOBY What is thy excellence in a galliard, knight?

SIR ANDREW Faith, I can cut a caper.

SIR TOBY And I can cut the mutton to't.

SIR ANDREW And I think I have the back-trick simply as strong as any man in Illyria.

SIR TOBY Wherefore are these things hid? wherefore have these gifts a curtain before 'em? are they like to take dust, like Mistress Mall's picture? why dost thou not go to church in a galliard and come home in a coranto? My very walk should be a jig; I would not so much as make water but in a sink-a-pace. What dost thou mean? Is it a world to hide virtues in?
I did think, by the excellent constitution of thy leg, it was formed under the star of a galliard.

SIR ANDREW Ay, 'tis strong, and it does indifferent well in a flame-coloured stock. Shall we set about some revels?

SIR TOBY What shall we do else? were we not born under Taurus?

SIR ANDREW Taurus! That's sides and heart.

托　　比	好得很，它披下来的样子就像纺杆上的麻线一样，我希望有哪位奶奶把你夹在大腿里纺它一纺。
安德鲁	真的，我明天要回家去了，托比爵士。你侄女不肯接见我；即使接见我，多半她也不会要我。这儿的公爵也向她求婚呢。
托　　比	她不要什么公爵不公爵；她不愿嫁给比她身份高、地位高、年龄高、智慧高的人，我听见她这样发过誓。嘿，老兄，还有希望呢。
安德鲁	我再耽搁一个月。我是世上心思最古怪的人；我有时老是喜欢喝酒跳舞。
托　　比	这种玩意儿你很擅胜场的吗，骑士？
安德鲁	可以比得过伊利里亚无论哪个不比我高明的人；可是我不愿跟老手比。
托　　比	你跳舞的本领怎样？
安德鲁	不骗你，我会旱地拔葱。
托　　比	我会葱炒羊肉。
安德鲁	讲到我的倒跳的本事，简直可以比得上伊利里亚的无论什么人。
托　　比	为什么你要把这种本领藏匿起来呢？为什么这种天才要覆上一块幕布？难道它们也会沾上灰尘，像大姑娘的画像一样吗？为什么不跳着"加里阿"到教堂里去，跳着"科兰多"一路回家？假如是我的话，我要走步路也是"捷格"舞，撒泡尿也是五步舞呢。你是什么意思？这世界上是应该把才能隐藏起来的吗？照你那双出色的好腿看来，我想它们是在一个跳舞的星光底下生下来的。
安德鲁	哦，我这双腿很有气力，穿了火黄色的袜子倒也十分漂亮。我们喝酒去吧？
托　　比	除了喝酒，咱们还有什么事好做？咱们的命宫不是金牛星吗？

SIR TOBY No, sir; it is legs and thighs. Let me see the caper; ha! higher: ha, ha! excellent!

Exeunt.

安 德 鲁　　金牛星!金牛星管的是腰和心。
托　　比　　不,老兄,是腿和股。跳个舞给我看。哈哈!跳得高些!哈哈!好极了!

　　　　　　　　　　同下。

SCENE IV

A room in DUKE ORSINO's palace.
Enter VALENTINE and VIOLA in man's attire.

VALENTINE If the duke continue these favours towards you, Cesario, you are like to be much advanced: he hath known you but three days, and already you are no stranger.

VIOLA You either fear his humour or my negligence, that you call in question the continuance of his love: is he inconstant, sir, in his favours?

VALENTINE No, believe me.

VIOLA I thank you. Here comes the count.

Enter DUKE ORSINO, CURIO, and Attendants.

DUKE Who saw Cesario, ho?

VIOLA On your attendance, my lord; here.

DUKE Stand you a while aloof, Cesario,
Thou know'st no less but all; I have unclasp'd
To thee the book even of my secret soul:
Therefore, good youth, address thy gait unto her;
Be not denied access, stand at her doors,
And tell them, there thy fixed foot shall grow
Till thou have audience.

VIOLA Sure, my noble lord,
If she be so abandon'd to her sorrow
As it is spoke, she never will admit me.

DUKE Be clamorous and leap all civil bounds
Rather than make unprofited return.

VIOLA Say I do speak with her, my lord, what then?

DUKE O, then unfold the passion of my love,
Surprise her with discourse of my dear faith:

第四场

公爵府中一室。
凡伦丁及薇奥拉男装上。

凡伦丁　要是公爵继续这样宠幸你，西萨里奥，你多半就要高升起来了；他认识你还只有三天，你就跟他这样熟了。

薇奥拉　看来你不是怕他的心性捉摸不定，就是怕我会玩忽职守，所以你才怀疑他会不会继续这样宠幸我。先生，他待人是不是有始无终的？

凡伦丁　不，相信我。

薇奥拉　谢谢你。公爵来了。

公爵，丘里奥及侍从等上。

公　爵　喂！有谁看见西萨里奥吗？

薇奥拉　在这儿，殿下，听候您的吩咐。

公　爵　你们暂时走开些。西萨里奥，你已经知道了一切，我已经把我内心中的秘密书册向你展示过了；因此，好孩子，到她那边去，别让他们把你摈之门外，站在她的门口，对他们说，你要站到脚底下生了根，直等她把你延见为止。

薇奥拉　殿下，要是她真像人家所说的那样沉浸在悲哀里，她一定不会允许我进去的。

公　爵　你可以跟他们吵闹，不用顾虑一切礼貌的界限，但一定不要毫无结果而归。

薇奥拉　假定我能够和她见面谈话了，殿下，那么又怎样呢？

公　爵　噢！那么就向她宣布我的恋爱的热情，把我的一片挚诚说给她听，让她吃惊。你表演起我的伤心来一定很出色，你这样的青年

	It shall become thee well to act my woes;
	She will attend it better in thy youth
	Than in a nuncio's of more grave aspect.
VIOLA	I think not so, my lord.
DUKE	Dear lad, believe it;
	For they shall yet belie thy happy years,
	That say thou art a man: Diana's lip
	Is not more smooth and rubious; thy small pipe
	Is as the maiden's organ, shrill and sound,
	And all is semblative a woman's part.
	I know thy constellation is right apt
	For this affair. Some four or five attend him;
	All, if you will; for I myself am best
	When least in company. Prosper well in this,
	And thou shalt live as freely as thy lord,
	To call his fortunes thine.
VIOLA	I'll do my best
	To woo your lady:
	[Aside] yet, a barful strife!
	Whoe'er I woo, myself would be his wife.

Exeunt.

一定比那些面孔板板的使者们更能引起她的注意。

薇奥拉　我想不见得吧，殿下。
公　爵　好孩子，相信我的话；因为像你这样的妙龄，还不能算是个成人：狄安娜的嘴唇也不比你的更柔滑而红润；你的娇细的喉咙像处女一样尖锐而清朗；在各方面你都像个女人。我知道你的性格很容易对付这件事情。四五个人陪着他去；要是你们愿意，就全去也好；因为我欢喜孤寂。你倘能成功，那么你主人的财产你也可以有份。

薇奥拉　我愿意尽力去向您的爱人求婚。
　　　　（旁白）唉，怨只怨多阻碍的前程！
　　　　但我一定要做他的夫人。

各下。

SCENE V

A room in OLIVIA'S house.
Enter MARIA and Clown.

MARIA	Nay, either tell me where thou hast been, or I will not open my lips so wide as a bristle may enter in way of thy excuse: my lady will hang thee for thy absence.
Clown	Let her hang me: he that is well hanged in this world needs to fear no colours.
MARIA	Make that good.
Clown	He shall see none to fear.
MARIA	A good lenten answer: I can tell thee where that saying was born, of 'I fear no colours.'
Clown	Where, good Mistress Mary?
MARIA	In the wars; and that may you be bold to say in your foolery.
Clown	Well, God give them wisdom that have it; and those that are fools, let them use their talents.
MARIA	Yet you will be hanged for being so long absent; or, to be turned away, is not that as good as a hanging to you?
Clown	Many a good hanging prevents a bad marriage; and, for turning away, let summer bear it out.
MARIA	You are resolute, then?
Clown	Not so, neither; but I am resolved on two points.
MARIA	That if one break, the other will hold; or, if both break, your gaskins fall.
Clown	Apt, in good faith; very apt. Well, go thy way; if Sir Toby would leave drinking, thou wert as witty a piece of Eve's flesh as any in Illyria.
MARIA	Peace, you rogue, no more o' that. Here comes my lady: make your excuse wisely, you were best.

第五场

奥丽维娅宅中一室。
玛利娅及小丑上。

玛利娅 不,你要是不告诉我你到哪里去来,我便把我的嘴唇抿得紧紧的,连一根毛发也钻不进去,不替你说句好话。小姐因为你不在,要吊死你呢。

小　丑 让她吊死我吧;好好地吊死的人,在这世上可以不怕敌人。

玛利娅 把你的话解释解释。

小　丑 因为他看不见敌人了。

玛利娅 好一句无聊的回答。让我告诉你"不怕敌人"这句话是怎么来的吧。

小　丑 怎么来的,玛利娅姑娘?

玛利娅 是从打仗里来的;下回你再撒赖的时候,就可以放开胆子这样说。

小　丑 好吧,上帝给聪明与聪明人;至于傻子们呢,那只好靠他们的本事了。

玛利娅 可是你这么久在外边鬼混,小姐一定要把你吊死的,否则把你赶出去,那不是跟把你吊死一样好吗?

小　丑 好好地吊死常常可以防止坏的婚姻;至于赶出去,那在夏天倒还没甚要紧。

玛利娅 那么你已经下了决心了吗?

小　丑 不,没有;可是我决定了两端。

玛利娅 假如一端断了,一端还连着;假如两端都断了,你的裤子也落下来了。

小　丑 妙,真的很妙。好,去你的吧;要是托比老爷戒了酒,你在伊利里亚的雌儿中间也好算是个门当户对的调皮角色了。

玛利娅 闭嘴,你这坏蛋,别胡说了。小姐来啦,你还是好好地想出个推托来。

Exit.

Clown   Wit, an't be thy will, put me into good fooling!

Those wits, that think they have thee, do very oft prove fools; and I, that am sure I lack thee, may pass for a wise man: for what says Quinapalus?

'Better a witty fool, than a foolish wit.'

Enter OLIVIA with MALVOLIO.

Clown   God bless thee, lady!

OLIVIA   Take the fool away.

Clown   Do you not hear, fellows? Take away the lady.

OLIVIA   Go to, you're a dry fool; I'll no more of you: besides, you grow dishonest.

Clown   Two faults, madonna, that drink and good counsel will amend: for give the dry fool drink, then is the fool not dry: bid the dishonest man mend himself; if he mend, he is no longer dishonest; if he cannot, let the botcher mend him. Any thing that's mended is but patched: virtue that transgresses is but patched with sin; and sin that amends is but patched with virtue. If that this simple syllogism will serve, so; if it will not, what remedy? As there is no true cuckold but calamity, so beauty's a flower. The lady bade take away the fool; therefore, I say again, take her away.

OLIVIA   Sir, I bade them take away you.

Clown   Misprision in the highest degree! Lady, cucullus non facit monachum; that's as much to say as I wear not motley in my brain. Good madonna, give me leave to prove you a fool.

OLIVIA   Can you do it?

Clown   Dexterously, good madonna.

下。

小　　丑　　才情呀，请你帮我好好地装一下傻瓜！那些自负才情的人，实际上往往是些傻瓜；我知道我自己没有才情，因此也许可以算做聪明人。昆那拍勒斯①怎么说的？"与其做愚蠢的智人，不如做聪明的愚人。"

　　　　　　　　　　奥丽维娅偕马伏里奥上。

小　　丑　　上帝祝福你，小姐！
奥丽维娅　　把这傻子撵出去！
小　　丑　　喂，你们不听见吗？把这位小姐撵出去。
奥丽维娅　　算了吧！你是个干燥无味的傻子，我不要再看见你了；而且你已经变得不老实起来了。
小　　丑　　我的小姐，这两个毛病用酒和忠告都可以治好。只要给干燥无味的傻子一点酒喝，他就不干燥了。只要劝不老实的人洗心革面，弥补他从前的过失：假如他能够弥补的话，他就不再不老实了；假如他不能弥补，那么叫裁缝把他补一补也就得了。弥补者，弥而补之也：道德的失足无非补上了一块罪恶；罪恶悔改之后，也无非补上了一块道德。假如这种简单的论理可以通得过去，很好；假如通不过去，还有什么办法？当王八是一件倒霉的事，美人好比鲜花，这都是无可怀疑的。小姐吩咐把傻子撵出去；因此我再说一句，把她撵出去吧。

奥丽维娅　　尊驾，我吩咐他们把你撵出去呢。
小　　丑　　这就是大错而特错了！小姐，"戴了和尚帽，不定是和尚"；那就好比是说，我身上虽然穿着愚人的彩衣，可是我并不一定连头脑里也穿着它呀。我的好小姐，准许我证明您是个傻子。
奥丽维娅　　你能吗？
小　　丑　　再便当也没有了，我的好小姐。

---

① 似为杜撰的人名。

OLIVIA	Make your proof.
Clown	I must catechise you for it, madonna: good my mouse of virtue, answer me.
OLIVIA	Well, sir, for want of other idleness, I'll bide your proof.
Clown	Good madonna, why mournest thou?
OLIVIA	Good fool, for my brother's death.
Clown	I think his soul is in hell, madonna.
OLIVIA	I know his soul is in heaven, fool.
Clown	The more fool, madonna, to mourn for your brother's soul being in heaven. Take away the fool, gentlemen.
OLIVIA	What think you of this fool, Malvolio? doth he not mend?
MALVOLIO	Yes, and shall do till the pangs of death shake him: infirmity, that decays the wise, doth ever make the better fool.
Clown	God send you, sir, a speedy infirmity, for the better increasing your folly! Sir Toby will be sworn that I am no fox; but he will not pass his word for two pence that you are no fool.
OLIVIA	How say you to that, Malvolio?
MALVOLIO	I marvel your ladyship takes delight in such a barren rascal: I saw him put down the other day with an ordinary fool that has no more brain than a stone. Look you now, he's out of his guard already; unless you laugh and minister occasion to him, he is gagged. I protest, I take these wise men, that crow so at these set kind of fools, no better than the fools' zanies.
OLIVIA	O, you are sick of self-love, Malvolio, and taste with a distempered appetite. To be generous, guiltless and of free disposition, is to take those things for bird-bolts that you deem cannon-bullets: there is no slander in an allowed fool, though he do nothing but rail; nor no railing in a known discreet man, though he do nothing but reprove.
Clown	Now Mercury endue thee with leasing, for thou speakest well of fools!

奥丽维娅　　那么证明一下看。
小　　丑　　小姐，我必须把您盘问；我的贤淑的小乖乖，回答我。

奥丽维娅　　好吧，先生，为了没有别的消遣，我就等候着你的证明吧。
小　　丑　　我的好小姐，你为什么悲伤？
奥丽维娅　　好傻子，为了我哥哥的死。
小　　丑　　小姐，我想他的灵魂是在地狱里。
奥丽维娅　　傻子，我知道他的灵魂是在天上。
小　　丑　　这就越显得你的傻了，我的小姐；你哥哥的灵魂既然在天上，为什么要悲伤呢？列位，把这傻子撵出去。
奥丽维娅　　马伏里奥，你以为这傻子怎样？是不是更有趣了？
马伏里奥　　是的，而且会变得越来越有趣，一直到死。老弱会使聪明减退，可是对于傻子却能使他变得格外傻起来。
小　　丑　　大爷，上帝保佑您快快老弱起来，好让您格外傻得厉害！托比老爷可以发誓说我不是狐狸，可是他不愿跟人家打赌两便士说您不是个傻子。
奥丽维娅　　你怎么说，马伏里奥？
马伏里奥　　我不懂您小姐怎么会喜欢这种没有头脑的混账东西。前天我看见他给一个像石头一样冥顽不灵的下等的傻子算计了去。您瞧，他已经毫无招架之功了；要是您不笑笑给他一点题目，他便要无话可说。我说，听见这种傻子的话也会那么高兴的聪明人们，都不过是些傻子们的应声虫罢了。

奥丽维娅　　啊！你是太自命不凡了，马伏里奥；你缺少一副健全的胃口。你认为是炮弹的，在宽容慷慨、气度汪洋的人看来，不过是鸟箭。傻子有特许放肆的权利，虽然他满口骂人，人家不会见怪于他；君子出言必有分量，虽然他老是指责人家的错处，也不能算为谩骂。

小　　丑　　麦鸠利赏给你说谎的本领吧，因为你给傻子说了好话！

Re-enter MARIA.

MARIA	Madam, there is at the gate a young gentleman much desires to speak with you.
OLIVIA	From the Count Orsino, is it?
MARIA	I know not, madam: 'tis a fair young man, and well attended.
OLIVIA	Who of my people hold him in delay?
MARIA	Sir Toby, madam, your kinsman.
OLIVIA	Fetch him off, I pray you; he speaks nothing but madman: fie on him!

Exit MARIA.

Go you, Malvolio: if it be a suit from the count, I am sick, or not at home; what you will, to dismiss it.

Exit MALVOLIO.

Now you see, sir, how your fooling grows old, and people dislike it.

Clown	Thou hast spoke for us, madonna, as if thy eldest son should be a fool; whose skull Jove cram with brains! for,— here he comes,—one of thy kin has a most weak pia mater.

Enter SIR TOBY BELCH.

OLIVIA	By mine honour, half drunk. What is he at the gate, cousin?
SIR TOBY	A gentleman.
OLIVIA	A gentleman! what gentleman?
SIR TOBY	'Tis a gentle man here—a plague o' these pickle-herring! How now, sot!
Clown	Good Sir Toby!
OLIVIA	Cousin, cousin, how have you come so early by this lethargy?
SIR TOBY	Lechery! I defy lechery. There's one at the gate.

玛利娅重上。

玛 利 娅 小姐，门口有一位年轻的先生很想见您说话。

奥丽维娅 从奥西诺公爵那儿来的吧？
玛 利 娅 我不知道，小姐；他是一位漂亮的青年，随从很盛。
奥丽维娅 我家里有谁在跟他周旋呢？
玛 利 娅 是令亲托比老爷，小姐。
奥丽维娅 你去叫他走开；他满口都是些疯话。不害羞的！

玛利娅下。

马伏里奥，你给我去；假若是公爵差来的，说我病了，或是不在家，随你怎样说，把他打发走。

马伏里奥下。

你瞧，先生，你的打诨已经陈腐起来，人家不喜欢了。

小　　丑 我的小姐，你帮我说话就像你的大儿子也会是个傻子一般；愿上帝在他的头颅里塞满脑子吧！瞧你的那位有一副最不中用的头脑的令亲来了。

托比·培尔契爵士上。

奥丽维娅 哎哟，又已经半醉了。叔叔，门口是谁？
托　比 一个绅士。
奥丽维娅 一个绅士！什么绅士？
托　比 有一个绅士在这儿——这种该死的咸鱼！怎样，蠢货！

小　　丑 好托比爷爷！
奥丽维娅 叔叔，叔叔，你怎么这么早就昏天黑地了？
托　比 声天色地！我打倒声天色地！有一个人在门口。

OLIVIA	Ay, marry, what is he?
SIR TOBY	Let him be the devil, an he will, I care not: give me faith, say I. Well, it's all one.

Exit.

OLIVIA	What's a drunken man like, fool?
Clown	Like a drowned man, a fool and a mad man: one draught above heat makes him a fool; the second mads him; and a third drowns him.
OLIVIA	Go thou and seek the crowner, and let him sit o' my coz; for he's in the third degree of drink, he's drowned: go, look after him.
Clown	He is but mad yet, madonna; and the fool shall look to the madman.

Exit.
Re-enter MALVOLIO.

MALVOLIO	Madam, yond young fellow swears he will speak with you. I told him you were sick; he takes on him to understand so much, and therefore comes to speak with you. I told him you were asleep; he seems to have a foreknowledge of that too, and therefore comes to speak with you. What is to be said to him, lady? he's fortified against any denial.
OLIVIA	Tell him he shall not speak with me.
MALVOLIO	Has been told so; and he says, he'll stand at your door like a sheriff's post, and be the supporter to a bench, but he'll speak with you.
OLIVIA	What kind o' man is he?
MALVOLIO	Why, of mankind.
OLIVIA	What manner of man?
MALVOLIO	Of very ill manner; he'll speak with you, will you or no.

奥丽维娅　是呀,他是谁呢?
托　比　　让他是魔鬼也好,我不管;我说,我心里耿耿三尺有神明。好,都是一样。

下。

奥丽维娅　傻子,醉汉像个什么东西?
小　丑　　像个溺死鬼,像个傻瓜,又像个疯子。多喝了一口就会把他变成个傻瓜;再喝一口就发了疯;喝了第三口就把他溺死了。

奥丽维娅　你去找个验尸的来吧,让他来验验我的叔叔;因为他已经喝酒喝到了第三个阶段,他已经溺死了。瞧瞧他去。

小　丑　　他还不过是发疯呢,我的小姐;傻子该去照顾疯子。

下。
马伏里奥重上。

马伏里奥　小姐,那个少年发誓说要见您说话。我对他说您有病;他说他知道,因此要来见您说话。我对他说您睡了;他似乎也早已知道了,因此要来见您说话。还有什么话好对他说呢,小姐?什么拒绝都挡他不了。

奥丽维娅　对他说我不要见他说话。
马伏里奥　这也已经对他说过了;他说,他要像州官衙门前竖着的旗杆那样立在您的门前不去,像凳子脚一样直挺挺地站着,非得见您说话不可。
奥丽维娅　他是怎样一个人?
马伏里奥　呃,就像一个人那么的。
奥丽维娅　可是是什么样子的呢?
马伏里奥　很无礼的样子;不管您愿不愿意,他一定要见您说话。

OLIVIA	Of what personage and years is he?
MALVOLIO	Not yet old enough for a man, nor young enough for a boy; as a squash is before 'tis a peascod, or a cooling when 'tis almost an apple: 'tis with him in standing water, between boy and man. He is very well-favoured and he speaks very shrewishly; one would think his mother's milk were scarce out of him.
OLIVIA	Let him approach: call in my gentlewoman.
MALVOLIO	Gentlewoman, my lady calls.

Exit.
Re-enter MARIA.

OLIVIA	Give me my veil: come, throw it o'er my face. We'll once more hear Orsino's embassy.

Enter VIOLA, and Attendants.

VIOLA	The honourable lady of the house, which is she?
OLIVIA	Speak to me; I shall answer for her. Your will?
VIOLA	Most radiant, exquisite and unmatchable beauty,—I pray you, tell me if this be the lady of the house, for I never saw her: I would be loath to cast away my speech, for besides that it is excellently well penned, I have taken great pains to con it. Good beauties, let me sustain no scorn; I am very comptible, even to the least sinister usage.
OLIVIA	Whence came you, sir?
VIOLA	I can say little more than I have studied, and that question's out of my part. Good gentle one, give me modest assurance if you be the lady of the house, that I may proceed in my speech.
OLIVIA	Are you a comedian?
VIOLA	No, my profound heart: and yet, by the very fangs of malice I swear, I am not that I play. Are you the lady of the house?

奥丽维娅　　他的相貌怎样？多大年纪？
马伏里奥　　说是个大人吧，年纪还太轻；说是个孩子吧，又嫌大些；就像是一颗没有成熟的豆荚，或是一只半生的苹果，又像大人又像小孩，所谓介乎两可之间。他长得很漂亮，说话也很刁钻；看他的样子，似乎有些未脱乳臭。

奥丽维娅　　叫他进来。把我的侍女唤来。
马伏里奥　　姑娘，小姐叫着你呢。

下。
玛利娅重上。

奥丽维娅　　把我的面纱拿来；来，罩住我的脸。我们要再听一次奥西诺来使的说话。

薇奥拉及侍从等上。

薇奥拉　　哪一位是这里府中的贵小姐？
奥丽维娅　　有什么话对我说吧；我可以代她答话。你来有什么见教？

薇奥拉　　最辉煌的、卓越的、无双的美人！请您指示我这位是不是就是这里府中的小姐，因为我没有见过她。我不大甘心滥掷我的言辞；因为它不但写得非常出色，而且我费了好大的辛苦才把它背熟。两位美人，不要把我取笑；我是个非常敏感的人，一点点轻侮都受不了的。

奥丽维娅　　你是从什么地方来的，先生？
薇奥拉　　除了我背熟了的以外，我不能说别的话；您那问题是我所不曾预备作答的。温柔的好人儿，好好儿地告诉我您是不是府里的小姐，好让我陈说我的来意。
奥丽维娅　　你是个唱戏的吗？
薇奥拉　　不，我的深心的人儿；可是我敢当着最有恶意的敌人发誓，我并不是我所扮演的角色。您是这府中的小姐吗？

OLIVIA	If I do not usurp myself, I am.
VIOLA	Most certain, if you are she, you do usurp yourself; for what is yours to bestow is not yours to reserve. But this is from my commission: I will on with my speech in your praise, and then show you the heart of my message.
OLIVIA	Come to what is important in't: I forgive you the praise.
VIOLA	Alas, I took great pains to study it, and 'tis poetical.
OLIVIA	It is the more like to be feigned: I pray you, keep it in. I heard you were saucy at my gates, and allowed your approach rather to wonder at you than to hear you. If you be not mad, be gone; if you have reason, be brief: 'tis not that time of moon with me to make one in so skipping a dialogue.
MARIA	Will you hoist sail, sir? here lies your way.
VIOLA	No, good swabber; I am to hull here a little longer. Some mollification for your giant, sweet lady.
OLIVIA	Tell me your mind:
VIOLA	I am a messenger.
OLIVIA	Sure, you have some hideous matter to deliver, when the courtesy of it is so fearful. Speak your office.
VIOLA	It alone concerns your ear. I bring no overture of war, no taxation of homage: I hold the olive in my hand; my words are as fun of peace as matter.
OLIVIA	Yet you began rudely. What are you? what would you?
VIOLA	The rudeness that hath appeared in me have I learned from my entertainment. What I am, and what I would, are as secret as maidenhead; to your ears, divinity, to any other's, profanation.
OLIVIA	Give us the place alone: we will hear this divinity.

Exeunt MARIA and Attendants.

Now, sir, what is your text?

奥丽维娅	是的,要是我没有篡夺了我自己。
薇奥拉	假如您就是她,那么您的确是篡夺了您自己了;因为您有权力给予别人的,您却没有权力把它藏匿起来。但是这种话跟我来此的使命无关;就要继续着恭维您的言辞,然后告知您我的来意。
奥丽维娅	把重要的话说出来;恭维免了吧。
薇奥拉	唉!我好容易才把它背熟,而且它又是很有诗意的。
奥丽维娅	那么多半是些鬼话,请你留着不用说了吧。我听说你在我门口一味顶撞;让你进来只是为要看看你究竟是个什么人,并不是要听你说话。要是你没有发疯,那么去吧;要是你明白事理,那么说得简单一些:我现在没有那样心思去理会一段没有意思的谈话。
玛利娅	请你动身吧,先生;这儿便是你的路。
薇奥拉	不,好清道夫,我还要在这儿闲荡一会儿呢。亲爱的小姐,请您劝劝您这位"彪形大汉"别那么神气活现。
奥丽维娅	把你的尊意告诉我。
薇奥拉	我是一个使者。
奥丽维娅	你那种礼貌那么可怕,你带来的信息一定是些坏事情。有什么话说出来。
薇奥拉	除了您之外不能让别人听见。我不是来向您宣战,也不是来要求您臣服;我手里握着橄榄枝,我的话里充满了和平,也充满了意义。
奥丽维娅	可是你一开始就不讲礼。你是谁?你要的是什么?
薇奥拉	我的不讲礼是我从你们对我的接待上学来的。我是谁,我要些什么,是个秘密;在您的耳中是神圣,别人听起来就是亵渎。
奥丽维娅	你们都走开吧;我们要听一听这段神圣的话。

玛利娅及侍从等下。

现在,先生,请教你的经文?

VIOLA	Most sweet lady,—
OLIVIA	A comfortable doctrine, and much may be said of it. Where lies your text?
VIOLA	In Orsino's bosom.
OLIVIA	In his bosom! In what chapter of his bosom?
VIOLA	To answer by the method, in the first of his heart.
OLIVIA	O, I have read it: it is heresy. Have you no more to say?
VIOLA	Good madam, let me see your face.
OLIVIA	Have you any commission from your lord to negotiate with my face? You are now out of your text: but we will draw the curtain and show you the picture.

She Unveils.

	Look you, sir, such a one I was this present: is't not well done?
VIOLA	Excellently done, if God did all.
OLIVIA	'Tis in grain, sir; 'twill endure wind and weather.
VIOLA	'Tis beauty truly blent, whose red and white Nature's own sweet and cunning hand laid on: Lady, you are the cruell'st she alive, If you will lead these graces to the grave And leave the world no copy.
OLIVIA	O, sir, I will not be so hard-hearted; I will give out divers schedules of my beauty: it shall be inventoried, and every particle and utensil labelled to my will: as, item, two lips, indifferent red; item, two grey eyes, with lids to them; item, one neck, one chin, and so forth. Were you sent hither to praise me?
VIOLA	I see you what you are, you are too proud; But, if you were the devil, you are fair. My lord and master loves you: O, such love

薇奥拉	最可爱的小姐——
奥丽维娅	倒是一种叫人听了怪舒服的教理，可以大发议论呢。你的经文呢？
薇奥拉	在奥西诺的心头。
奥丽维娅	在他的心头！在他的心头的哪一章？
薇奥拉	照目录上排起来，是他心头的第一章。
奥丽维娅	噢！那我已经读过了，无非是些旁门左道。你没有别的话要说了吗？
薇奥拉	好小姐，让我瞧瞧您的脸。
奥丽维娅	贵主人有什么事要差你来跟我的脸接洽的吗？你现在岔开你的正文了；可是我们不妨拉开幕儿，让你看看这幅图画。

揭除面幕。

你瞧，先生，我就是这个样子；它不是画得很好吗？
薇奥拉	要是一切都出于上帝的手，那真是绝妙之笔。
奥丽维娅	它的色彩很耐久，先生，受得起风霜的侵蚀。
薇奥拉	那真是各种色彩精妙地调和而成的美貌；那红红的白白的都是造化者亲自用他的可爱的巧手敷上去的。小姐，您是世上最狠心的女人，要是您甘心让这种美埋没在坟墓里，不给世间留下一份副本。

| 奥丽维娅 | 啊！先生，我不会那样狠心；我可以列下一张我的美貌的清单，一一开陈清楚，把每一件细目都载在我的遗嘱上，例如：一款，浓淡适中的朱唇两片；一款，灰色的倩眼一双，附眼睑；一款，玉颈一围，柔颐一个，等等。你是奉命到这儿来恭维我的吗？ |

| 薇奥拉 | 我明白您是个什么样的人了。您太骄傲了；可是即使您是个魔鬼，您是美貌的。我的主人爱着您；啊！这么一种爱情，即使您 |

	Could be but recompensed, though you were crown'd
	The nonpareil of beauty!
OLIVIA	How does he love me?
VIOLA	With adorations, fertile tears,
	With groans that thunder love, with sighs of fire.
OLIVIA	Your lord does know my mind; I cannot love him:
	Yet I suppose him virtuous, know him noble,
	Of great estate, of fresh and stainless youth;
	In voices well divulged, free, learn'd and valiant;
	And in dimension and the shape of nature
	A gracious person: but yet I cannot love him;
	He might have took his answer long ago.
VIOLA	If I did love you in my master's flame,
	With such a suffering, such a deadly life,
	In your denial I would find no sense;
	I would not understand it.
OLIVIA	Why, what would you?
VIOLA	Make me a willow cabin at your gate,
	And call upon my soul within the house;
	Write loyal cantons of contemned love
	And sing them loud even in the dead of night;
	Halloo your name to the reverberate hills
	And make the babbling gossip of the air
	Cry out 'Olivia!' O, You should not rest
	Between the elements of air and earth,
	But you should pity me!
OLIVIA	You might do much.
	What is your parentage?
VIOLA	Above my fortunes, yet my state is well:
	I am a gentleman.
OLIVIA	Get you to your lord;

是人间的绝色，也应该酬答他的。

奥丽维娅　他怎样爱着我呢？
薇奥拉　用崇拜，大量的眼泪，震响着爱情的呻吟，吞吐着烈火的叹息。
奥丽维娅　你的主人知道我的意思，我不能爱他；虽然我想他品格很高，知道他很尊贵，很有身份，年轻而纯洁，有很好的名声，慷慨，博学，勇敢，长得又体面；可是我总不能爱他，他老早就已经得到我的回音了。

薇奥拉　要是我也像我主人一样热情地爱着您，也是这样的受苦，这样了无生趣地把生命拖延，我不会懂得您的拒绝是什么意思。

奥丽维娅　啊，你预备怎样呢？
薇奥拉　我要在您的门前用柳枝筑成一所小屋，不时到府中访谒我的灵魂；我要吟咏着被冷淡的忠诚的爱情的篇什，不顾夜多么深我要把它们高声歌唱，我要向着回声的山崖呼喊您的名字，使饶舌的风都叫着"奥丽维娅"。啊！您在天地之间将要得不到安静，除非您怜悯了我！

奥丽维娅　你的口才倒是颇堪造就的。你的家世怎样？

薇奥拉　超过于我目前的境遇，但我是个有身份的士人。

奥丽维娅　回到你主人那里去；我不能爱他，叫他不要再差人来了；除非或

	I cannot love him: let him send no more;
	Unless, perchance, you come to me again,
	To tell me how he takes it. Fare you well:
	I thank you for your pains: spend this for me.
VIOLA	I am no fee'd post, lady; keep your purse:
	My master, not myself, lacks recompense.
	Love make his heart of flint that you shall love;
	And let your fervor, like my master's, be
	Placed in contempt! Farewell, fair cruelty.

Exit.

OLIVIA 'What is your parentage?'
'Above my fortunes, yet my state is well:
I am a gentleman.' I'll be sworn thou art;
Thy tongue, thy face, thy limbs, actions and spirit,
Do give thee five-fold blazon: not too fast: soft, soft!
Unless the master were the man. How now!
Even so quickly may one catch the plague?
Methinks I feel this youth's perfections
With an invisible and subtle stealth
To creep in at mine eyes. Well, let it be.
What ho, Malvolio!

Re-enter MALVOLIO.

MALVOLIO Here, madam, at your service.
OLIVIA Run after that same peevish messenger,
The county's man: he left this ring behind him,
Would I or not: tell him I'll none of it.
Desire him not to flatter with his lord,
Nor hold him up with hopes; I am not for him:

者你再来见我，告诉我他对于我的答复觉得怎样。再会！多谢你的辛苦；这几个钱赏给你。

薇奥拉　我不是个要钱的信差，小姐，留着您的钱吧；不曾得到报酬的，是我的主人，不是我。但愿爱神使您所爱的人也是心如铁石，好让您的热情也跟我主人的一样遭到轻蔑！再会，狠心的美人！

下。

奥丽维娅　"你的家世怎样？""超过于我目前的境遇，但我是个有身份的士人。"我可以发誓你一定是的；你的语调，你的脸，你的肢体、动作、精神，各方面都可以证明你的高贵。——别这么性急。且慢！且慢！除非颠倒了主仆的名分。——什么！这么快便染上那种病了？我觉得好像这个少年的美处在悄悄地蹑步进入我的眼中。好，让它去吧。喂！马伏里奥！

马伏里奥重上。

马伏里奥　有，小姐，听候您的吩咐。
奥丽维娅　去追上那个无礼的使者，公爵差来的人，他不管我要不要，硬把这戒指留下；对他说我不要，请他不要向他的主人献功，让他死不了心，我跟他没有缘分。要是那少年明天还打这儿走过，我可以告诉他为什么。去吧，马伏里奥。

If that the youth will come this way to-morrow,
I'll give him reasons for't: hie thee, Malvolio.

MALVOLIO Madam, I will.

Exit.

OLIVIA I do I know not wha t, and fear to find
Mine eye too great a flatterer for my mind.
Fate, show thy force: ourselves we do not owe;
What is decreed must be, and be this so!

Exit.

马伏里奥　　是,小姐。

　　　　　　　　　　　下。

奥丽维娅　　我的行事我自己全不懂,
　　　　　　　怎一下子便会把人看中?
　　　　　　　一切但凭着命运的吩咐,
　　　　　　　谁能够作得了自己的主!

　　　　　　　　　　　下。

ACT II 第二幕

SCENE I

The sea-coast.
Enter ANTONIO and SEBASTIAN.

ANTONIO Will you stay no longer? nor will you not that I go with you?

SEBASTIAN By your patience, no. My stars shine darkly over me: the malignancy of my fate might perhaps distemper yours; therefore I shall crave of you your leave that I may bear my evils alone: it were a bad recompense for your love, to lay any of them on you.

ANTONIO Let me yet know of you whither you are bound.

SEBASTIAN No, sooth, sir: my determinate voyage is mere extravagancy. But I perceive in you so excellent a touch of modesty, that you will not extort from me what I am willing to keep in; therefore it charges me in manners the rather to express myself. You must know of me then, Antonio, my name is Sebastian, which I called Roderigo. My father was that Sebastian of Messaline, whom I know you have heard of. He left behind him myself and a sister, both born in an hour: if the heavens had been pleased, would we had so ended! but you, sir, altered that; for some hour before you took me from the breach of the sea was my sister drowned.

ANTONIO Alas the day!

SEBASTIAN A lady, sir, though it was said she much resembled me, was yet of many accounted beautiful: but, though I could not with such estimable wonder overfar believe that, yet thus far I will boldly publish her; she bore a mind that envy could not but call fair. She is drowned already, sir, with salt water, though I seem to drown her remembrance again with more.

ANTONIO Pardon me, sir, your bad entertainment.

第一场

海滨。
安东尼奥及西巴斯辛上。

安东尼奥 您不愿住下去了吗?您也不愿让我陪着您去吗?

西巴斯辛 请您原谅,我不愿。我是个倒霉的人,我的晦气也许要连累了您,所以我要请您离开我,好让我独自承担我的厄运;假如连累到您身上,那是太辜负了您的好意了。

安东尼奥 可是让我知道您的去向吧。

西巴斯辛 不瞒您说,先生,我不能告诉您;因为我所决定的航行不过是无目的的漫游。可是我看您这样有礼,您一定不会强迫我说出我所保守的秘密来;因此按礼该我来向您表白我自己。安东尼奥,您要知道我的名字是西巴斯辛,罗德利哥是我的化名。我的父亲便是梅萨林的西巴斯辛,我知道您一定听见过他的名字。他死后丢下我和一个妹妹,我们两人是在同一个时辰出世的;我多么希望上天也让我们两人在同一个时辰死去!可是您,先生,却来改变我的命运,因为就在您把我从海浪里打救起来之前不久,我的妹妹已经淹死了。

安东尼奥 唉,可惜!

西巴斯辛 先生,虽然人家说她非常像我,许多人都说她是个美貌的姑娘;我虽然不好意思相信这句话,但是至少可以大胆说一句,即使妒忌她的人也不能不承认她有一颗美好的心。她是已经给海水淹死的了,先生,虽然似乎我要用更多的泪水来淹没对她的记忆。

安东尼奥 先生,请您恕我招待不周。

SEBASTIAN O good Antonio, forgive me your trouble.

ANTONIO If you will not murder me for my love, let me be your servant.

SEBASTIAN If you will not undo what you have done, that is, kill him whom you have recovered, desire it not.
Fare ye well at once: my bosom is full of kindness, and I am yet so near the manners of my mother, that upon the least occasion more mine eyes will tell tales of me. I am bound to the Count Orsino's court: farewell.

Exit.

ANTONIO The gentleness of all the gods go with thee!
I have many enemies in Orsino's court,
Else would I very shortly see thee there.
But, come what may, I do adore thee so,
That danger shall seem sport, and I will go.

Exit.

西巴斯辛	啊,好安东尼奥!我才是多多打扰了您哪!
安东尼奥	要是您看在我的交情分上,不愿叫我痛不欲生的话,请您允许我做您的仆人吧。
西巴斯辛	您已经搭救了我的生命,要是您不愿让我抱愧而死,那么请不要提出那样的请求,免得您白白救了我一场。我立刻告辞了!我的心是怪软的,还不曾脱去我母亲的性质,为了一点点理由,我的眼睛里就会露出我的弱点来。就要到奥西诺公爵的宫廷里去;再会了。

下。

安东尼奥	一切神明护佑着你!我在奥西诺的宫廷里有许多敌人,否则我就会马上到那边去会你—— 但无论如何我爱你太深, 履险如夷我定要把你寻。

下。

SCENE II

A street.
Enter VIOLA, MALVOLIO following.

MALVOLIO Were not you even now with the Countess Olivia?

VIOLA Even now, sir; on a moderate pace I have since arrived but hither.

MALVOLIO She returns this ring to you, sir: you might have saved me my pains, to have taken it away yourself.
She adds, moreover, that you should put your lord into a desperate assurance she will none of him: and one thing more, that you be never so hardy to come again in his affairs, unless it be to report your lord's taking of this. Receive it so.

VIOLA She took the ring of me: I'll none of it.

MALVOLIO Come, sir, you peevishly threw it to her; and her will is, it should be so returned: if it be worth stooping for, there it lies in your eye; if not, be it his that finds it.

Exit.

VIOLA I left no ring with her: what means this lady?
Fortune forbid my outside have not charm'd her!
She made good view of me; indeed, so much,
That sure methought her eyes had lost her tongue,
For she did speak in starts distractedly.
She loves me, sure; the cunning of her passion
Invites me in this churlish messenger.
None of my lord's ring! why, he sent her none.
I am the man: if it be so, as 'tis,
Poor lady, she were better love a dream.
Disguise, I see, thou art a wickedness,
Wherein the pregnant enemy does much.

第二场

街道。

薇奥拉上,马伏里奥随上。

马伏里奥　您不是刚从奥丽维娅伯爵小姐那儿来的吗?

薇奥拉　是的,先生;因为我走得慢,所以现在还不过在这儿。

马伏里奥　先生,这戒指她还给您;您当初还不如自己拿走呢,免得我麻烦。她又说您必须叫您家主人死了心,明白她不要跟他来往。还有,您不用再那么莽撞地到这里来替他说话了,除非来回报一声您家主人已经对她的拒绝表示认可。好,拿去吧。

薇奥拉　她自己拿了我这戒指去的;我不要。

马伏里奥　算了吧,先生,您使性子把它丢给她;她的意思也要我把它照样丢还给您。假如它是值得弯下身子拾起来的话,它就在您的眼前;不然的话,让什么人看见就给什么人拿去吧。

下。

薇奥拉　我没有留下戒指呀;这位小姐是什么意思?但愿她不要迷恋了我的外貌才好!她把我打量得那么仔细;真的,我觉得她看得我那么出神,连自己讲的什么话儿也顾不到了,那么没头没脑,颠颠倒倒的。一定的,她爱上我啦;情急智生,才差这个无礼的使者来邀请我。不要我主人的戒指!嘿,他并没有把什么戒指送给她呀!我才是她意中的人;真是这样的话——事实上确是这样——那么,可怜的小姐,她真是做梦了!我现在才明白假扮的确不是一桩好事情,魔鬼会乘机大显他的身手。一个又漂亮又靠不住的男人,多么容易占据了女人家柔弱的心!唉!这都是我们生性脆弱的缘故,不是我们自身的错处;因为上天造下我们是哪样的人,我们就是哪样的人。这种事情怎么了结呢?我的主人深深地爱着她;我呢,可怜的小鬼,也是那样恋着他;她呢,认错了

How easy is it for the proper-false
In women's waxen hearts to set their forms!
Alas, our frailty is the cause, not we!
For such as we are made of, such we be.
How will this fadge? my master loves her dearly;
And I, poor monster, fond as much on him;
And she, mistaken, seems to dote on me.
What will become of this? As I am man,
My state is desperate for my master's love;
As I am woman,—now alas the day!—
What thriftless sighs shall poor Olivia breathe!
O time! thou must untangle this, not I;
It is too hard a knot for me to untie!

Exit.

人，似乎在思念我。这怎么了呢？因为我是个男人，我没有希望叫我的主人爱上我；因为我是个女人，唉！可怜的奥丽维娅也要白费无数的叹息了！
这纠纷要让时间来理清；
叫我打开这结儿怎么成！

    下。

SCENE III

A room in OLIVIA's house.
Enter SIR TOBY BELCH and SIR ANDREW AGUECHEEK.

SIR TOBY   Approach, Sir Andrew: not to be abed after midnight is to be up betimes; and 'diluculo surgere,' thou know'st,—

SIR ANDREW   Nay, my troth, I know not: but I know, to be up late is to be up late.

SIR TOBY   A false conclusion: I hate it as an unfilled can. To be up after midnight and to go to bed then, is early: so that to go to bed after midnight is to go to bed betimes. Does not our life consist of the four elements?

SIR ANDREW   Faith, so they say; but I think it rather consists of eating and drinking.

SIR TOBY   Thou'rt a scholar; let us therefore eat and drink. Marian, I say! a stoup of wine!

Enter Clown.

SIR ANDREW   Here comes the fool, i' faith.

Clown   How now, my hearts! did you never see the picture of 'we three'?

SIR TOBY   Welcome, ass. Now let's have a catch.

SIR ANDREW   By my troth, the fool has an excellent breast. I had rather than forty shillings I had such a leg, and so sweet a breath to sing, as the fool has. In sooth, thou wast in very gracious fooling last night, when thou spokest of Pigrogromitus, of the Vapians passing the equinoctial of Queubus: 'twas very good, i' faith. I sent thee sixpence for thy leman: hadst it?

Clown   I did impeticos thy gratillity; for Malvolio's nose is no whipstock: my lady has a white hand, and the Myrmidons are no bottle-ale houses.

第三场

奥丽维娅宅中一室。

托比·培尔契爵士及安德鲁·艾古契克爵士上。

托　比	过来，安德鲁爵士。深夜不睡即是起身得早；"起身早，身体好"，你知道的——
安德鲁	不，老实说，我不知道；我知道的是深夜不睡便是深夜不睡。
托　比	一个错误的结论；我听见这种话就像看见一个空酒瓶那么头痛。深夜不睡，过了半夜才睡，那就是到大清早才睡，岂不是睡得很早？我们的生命不是由四大元素组成的吗？
安德鲁	不错，他们是这样说；可是我以为我们的生命不过是吃吃喝喝而已。
托　比	你真有学问；那么让我们吃吃喝喝吧。玛利娅，喂！开一瓶酒来！

小丑上。

安德鲁	那个傻子来啦。
小　丑	啊，我的心肝们！咱们刚好凑成一幅《三个臭皮匠》。
托　比	欢迎，驴子！现在我们来一个轮唱歌吧。
安德鲁	说老实话，这傻子有一副很好的喉咙。我宁愿拿四十个先令去换他这么一条腿和这么一副可爱的声音。真的，你昨夜打诨打得很好，说什么匹格罗格罗密忒斯哪维比亚人越过了丘勃斯的赤道线哪，真是好得很。我送六便士给你的姘头，收到了没有？
小　丑	你的恩典我已经放进了我的口袋；因为马伏里奥的鼻子不是鞭柄，我的小姐有一双玉手，她的跟班们不是开酒馆的。

SIR ANDREW Excellent! why, this is the best fooling, when all is done. Now, a song.
SIR TOBY Come on; there is sixpence for you: let's have a song.
SIR ANDREW There's a testril of me too: if one knight give a—
Clown Would you have a love-song, or a song of good life?
SIR TOBY A love-song, a love-song.
SIR ANDREW Ay, ay: I care not for good life.
Clown *[Sings]*

O mistress mine, where are you roaming?

O, stay and hear; your true love's coming,

That can sing both high and low:

Trip no further, pretty sweeting;

Journeys end in lovers meeting,

Every wise man's son doth know.

SIR ANDREW Excellent good, i' faith.
SIR TOBY Good, good.
Clown *[Sings]*

What is love? 'tis not hereafter;

Present mirth hath present laughter;

What's to come is still unsure:

In delay there lies no plenty;

Then come kiss me, sweet and twenty,

Youth's a stuff will not endure.

SIR ANDREW A mellifluous voice, as I am true knight.
SIR TOBY A contagious breath.
SIR ANDREW Very sweet and contagious, i' faith.
SIR TOBY To hear by the nose, it is dulcet in contagion. But shall we make the welkin dance indeed? shall we rouse the night-owl in a catch that will draw three souls out of one weaver? shall we do that?
SIR ANDREW An you love me, let's do't: I am dog at a catch.

安德鲁　　好极了！嗯，无论如何这要算是最好的打诨了。现在唱个歌吧。
托　比　　来，给你六便士，唱个歌吧。
安德鲁　　我也有六便士给你呢；要是一个骑士大方起来——

小　丑　　你们要我唱支爱情的歌呢，还是唱支劝人为善的歌？
托　比　　唱个情歌，唱个情歌。
安德鲁　　是的，是的，劝人为善有什么意思。
小　丑　　（唱）
　　　　　你到哪儿去，啊我的姑娘？
　　　　　听呀，那边来了你的情郎，
　　　　　嘴里吟着抑扬的曲调。
　　　　　不要再走了，美貌的亲亲；
　　　　　恋人的相遇终结了行程，
　　　　　每个聪明人全都知晓。

安德鲁　　真好极了！
托　比　　好，好！
小　丑　　（唱）
　　　　　什么是爱情？它不在明天；
　　　　　欢笑嬉游莫放过了眼前，
　　　　　将来的事有谁能猜料？
　　　　　不要蹉跎了大好的年华；
　　　　　来吻着我吧，你双十娇娃，
　　　　　转眼青春早化成衰老。

安德鲁　　凭良心说话，好一副流利的歌喉！
托　比　　好一股恶臭的气息！
安德鲁　　真的，很甜蜜又很恶臭。
托　比　　用鼻子听起来，那么恶臭也很动听。可是我们要不要让天空跳起舞来呢？我们要不要唱一支轮唱歌，把夜枭吵醒；那曲调会叫一个织工听了三魂出窍？

安德鲁　　要是你爱我，让我们来一下吧；唱轮唱歌我挺拿手啦。

Clown	By'r lady, sir, and some dogs will catch well.
SIR ANDREW	Most certain. Let our catch be, 'Thou knave.'
Clown	'Hold thy peace, thou knave,' knight? I shall be constrained in't to call thee knave, knight.
SIR ANDREW	'Tis not the first time I have constrained one to call me knave. Begin, fool: it begins 'Hold thy peace.'
Clown	I shall never begin if I hold my peace.
SIR ANDREW	Good, i' faith. Come, begin.

Catch sung.
Enter MARIA.

MARIA	What a caterwauling do you keep here! If my lady have not called up her steward Malvolio and bid him turn you out of doors, never trust me.
SIR TOBY	My lady's a Cataian, we are politicians, Malvolio's a Peg-a-Ramsey, and 'Three merry men be we.' Am not I consanguineous? am I not of her blood? Tillyvally. Lady! [*Sings*] 'There dwelt a man in Babylon, lady, lady!'
Clown	Beshrew me, the knight's in admirable fooling.
SIR ANDREW	Ay, he does well enough if he be disposed, and so do I too: he does it with a better grace, but I do it more natural.
SIR TOBY	[*Sings*] 'O, the twelfth day of December,'—
MARIA	For the love o' God, peace!

Enter MALVOLIO.

MALVOLIO	My masters, are you mad? or what are you? Have ye no wit, manners, nor honesty, but to gabble like tinkers at this time of night? Do ye make an alehouse of my lady's house, that ye squeak out your coziers' catches without any mitigation or

小　　　丑　　对啦，大人，有许多狗也会唱得很好。

安 德 鲁　　不错不错。让我们唱《你这坏蛋》吧。

小　　　丑　　《闭住你的嘴，你这坏蛋》，是不是这一首，骑士？那么我可不得不叫你做坏蛋啦，骑士。

安 德 鲁　　人家不得不叫我做坏蛋，这也不是第一次。你开头，傻子；第一句是，"闭住你的嘴。"

小　　　丑　　要是我闭住我的嘴，我就再也开不了头啦。

安 德 鲁　　说得好，真的。来，唱起来吧。

　　　　　　　　　　三人唱轮唱歌。
　　　　　　　　　　玛利娅上。

玛 利 娅　　你们在这里猫儿叫春似的闹些什么呀！要是小姐没有叫起她的管家马伏里奥来把你们赶出门外去，再不用相信我的话好了。

托　　　比　　小姐是个骗子；我们都是大人物；马伏里奥是拉姆西的佩格姑娘；"我们是三个快活的人"。我不是同宗吗？我不是她的一家人吗？胡说八道，姑娘！巴比伦有一个人，姑娘，姑娘！

小　　　丑　　要命，这位老爷真会开玩笑。

安 德 鲁　　哦，他高兴开起玩笑来，开得可是真好，我也一样；不过他的玩笑开得富于风趣，而我的玩笑开得更为自然。

托　　　比　　（唱）啊！十二月十二——

玛 利 娅　　看在上帝的面上，别闹了吧！

　　　　　　　　　　马伏里奥上。

马伏里奥　　我的爷爷们，你们疯了吗，还是怎么啦？难道你们没有脑子，不懂规矩，全无礼貌，在这种夜深时候还要像一群发酒疯的补锅匠似的乱吵？你们把小姐的屋子当作一间酒馆，好让你们直着喉咙，唱那种鞋匠的歌儿吗？难道你们全不想想这是什么地方，

	remorse of voice? Is there no respect of place, persons, nor time in you?
SIR TOBY	We did keep time, sir, in our catches. Sneck up!
MALVOLIO	Sir Toby, I must be round with you. My lady bade me tell you, that, though she harbours you as her kinsman, she's nothing allied to your disorders. If you can separate yourself and your misdemeanors, you are welcome to the house; if not, an it would please you to take leave of her, she is very willing to bid you farewell.
SIR TOBY	'Farewell, dear heart, since I must needs be gone.'
MARIA	Nay, good Sir Toby.
Clown	'His eyes do show his days are almost done.'
MALVOLIO	Is't even so?
SIR TOBY	'But I will never die.'
Clown	Sir Toby, there you lie.
MALVOLIO	This is much credit to you.
SIR TOBY	'Shall I bid him go?'
Clown	'What an if you do?'
SIR TOBY	'Shall I bid him go, and spare not?'
Clown	'O no, no, no, no, you dare not.'
SIR TOBY	Out o' tune, sir: ye lie. Art any more than a steward? Dost thou think, because thou art virtuous, there shall be no more cakes and ale?
Clown	Yes, by Saint Anne, and ginger shall be hot i' the mouth too.
SIR TOBY	Thou'rt i' the right. Go, sir, rub your chain with crumbs. A stoup of wine, Maria!
MALVOLIO	Mistress Mary, if you prized my lady's favour at any thing more than contempt, you would not give means for this uncivil rule: she shall know of it, by this hand.

Exit.

这儿住的是什么人，或者现在是什么时刻了吗？

托　　比　　老兄，我们的轮唱是严守时刻的。你去上吊吧！
马伏里奥　　托比老爷，莫怪我说句不怕忌讳的话。小姐吩咐我告诉您说，她虽然把您当个亲戚留住在这儿，可是她不能容忍您那种胡闹。要是您能够循规蹈矩，我们这儿是十分欢迎您的；否则的话，要是您愿意向她告别，她一定会让您走。

托　　比　　既然我非去不可，那么再会吧，亲亲！
玛　利　娅　　别这样，好托比老爷。
小　　丑　　他的眼睛显示出他末日将要来临。
马伏里奥　　岂有此理！
托　　比　　可是我决不会死亡。
小　　丑　　托比老爷，您在说谎。
马伏里奥　　真有体统！
托　　比　　我要不要叫他滚蛋？
小　　丑　　叫他滚蛋又怎样？
托　　比　　要不要叫他滚蛋，毫无留贷？
小　　丑　　啊！不，不，不，你没有这种胆量。
托　　比　　唱的不入调吗？先生，你说谎！你不过是一个管家，有什么可以神气的？你以为你自己道德高尚，人家便不能喝酒取乐了吗？

小　　丑　　是啊，凭圣安起誓，生姜吃下嘴去也总是辣的。
托　　比　　你说得一点也不错。——去，朋友，用面包屑去擦你的项链吧。开一瓶酒来，玛利娅！
马伏里奥　　玛利娅姑娘，要是你没有把小姐的恩典看作一钱不值，你可不要帮助他们做这种胡闹；我一定会去告诉她的。

下。

MARIA Go shake your ears.

SIR ANDREW 'Twere as good a deed as to drink when a man's a-hungry, to challenge him the field, and then to break promise with him and make a fool of him.

SIR TOBY Do't, knight: I'll write thee a challenge: or I'll deliver thy indignation to him by word of mouth.

MARIA Sweet Sir Toby, be patient for tonight: since the youth of the count's was today with thy lady, she is much out of quiet. For Monsieur Malvolio, let me alone with him: if I do not gull him into a nayword, and make him a common recreation, do not think I have wit enough to lie straight in my bed: I know I can do it.

SIR TOBY Possess us, possess us; tell us something of him.

MARIA Marry, sir, sometimes he is a kind of puritan.

SIR ANDREW O, if I thought that I'ld beat him like a dog!

SIR TOBY What, for being a puritan? thy exquisite reason, dear knight?

SIR ANDREW I have no exquisite reason for't, but I have reason good enough.

MARIA The devil a puritan that he is, or any thing constantly, but a time-pleaser; an affectioned ass, that cons state without book and utters it by great swarths: the best persuaded of himself, so crammed, as he thinks, with excellencies, that it is his grounds of faith that all that look on him love him; and on that vice in him will my revenge find notable cause to work.

SIR TOBY What wilt thou do?

MARIA I will drop in his way some obscure epistles of love; wherein, by the colour of his beard, the shape of his leg, the manner of his gait, the expressure of his eye, forehead, and complexion, he shall find himself most feelingly personated. I can write very like my lady your niece: on a forgotten matter we can hardly make distinction of our hands.

SIR TOBY Excellent! I smell a device.

玛利娅　　滚你的吧!

安德鲁　　向他挑战,然后失约,愚弄他一下子,倒是个很好的办法,就像人肚子饿了喝酒一样。

托　比　　好,骑士,我给你写挑战书,或者代你去口头通知他你的愤怒。

玛利娅　　亲爱的托比老爷,今夜请忍耐一下子吧;今天公爵那边来的少年会见了小姐之后,她心里很烦。至于马伏里奥先生,我去对付他好了;要是我不把他愚弄得给人当作笑柄,让大家取乐儿,我便是个连直挺挺躺在床上都不会的蠢东西。我知道我一定能够。

托　比　　告诉我们,告诉我们;告诉我们一些关于他的事情。

玛利娅　　好,老爷,有时候他有点儿像清教徒。

安德鲁　　啊!要是我早想到了这一点,我要把他像狗一样打一顿呢。

托　比　　什么,为了像清教徒吗?你有什么绝妙的理由,亲爱的骑士?

安德鲁　　我没有什么绝妙的理由,可是我有相当的理由。

玛利娅　　他是个鬼清教徒,反复无常、逢迎取巧是他的本领;一头装腔作势的驴子,背熟了几句官话,便倒也似的倒了出来;自信非凡,以为自己真了不得,谁看见他都会爱他;我可以凭着那个弱点堂堂正正地给他一顿教训。

托　比　　你打算怎样?

玛利娅　　我要在他走过的路上丢了一封暧昧的情书,里面活生生地描写着他的胡须的颜色、他的腿的形状、他走路的姿势、他的眼睛、额角和脸上的表情;他一见就会觉得是写的他自己。我会学您侄小姐的笔迹写字;在已经忘记了的信件上,我们连自己的笔迹也很难辨认呢。

托　比　　好极了,我嗅到了一个计策了。

SIR ANDREW I have't in my nose too.

SIR TOBY He shall think, by the letters that thou wilt drop, that they come from my niece, and that she's in love with him.

MARIA My purpose is, indeed, a horse of that colour.

SIR ANDREW And your horse now would make him an ass.

MARIA Ass, I doubt not.

SIR ANDREW O, 'twill be admirable!

MARIA Sport royal, I warrant you: I know my physic will work with him. I will plant you two, and let the fool make a third, where he shall find the letter: observe his construction of it. For this night, to bed, and dream on the event. Farewell.

Exit.

SIR TOBY Good night, Penthesilea.

SIR ANDREW Before me, she's a good wench.

SIR TOBY She's a beagle, true-bred, and one that adores me: what o' that?

SIR ANDREW I was adored once too.

SIR TOBY Let's to bed, knight. Thou hadst need send for more money.

SIR ANDREW If I cannot recover your niece, I am a foul way out.

SIR TOBY Send for money, knight: if thou hast her not i' the end, call me cut.

SIR ANDREW If I do not, never trust me, take it how you will.

SIR TOBY Come, come, I'll go burn some sack; 'tis too late to go to bed now: come, knight; come, knight.

Exeunt.

安 德 鲁　　我鼻子里也闻到了呢。

托　　比　　他见了你丢下的这封信，便会以为是我的侄女写的，以为她爱上了他。

玛 利 娅　　我的意思正是这样。

安 德 鲁　　你的意思是要叫他变成一头驴子。

玛 利 娅　　驴子，那是毫无疑问的。

安 德 鲁　　啊！那好极了！

玛 利 娅　　出色的把戏，你们瞧着好了；我知道我的药对他一定生效。我可以把你们两人连那傻子安顿在他拾着那信的地方，瞧他怎样把它解释。今夜呢，大家上床睡去，梦着那回事吧。再见。

下。

托　　比　　晚安，好姑娘！

安 德 鲁　　我说，她是个好丫头。

托　　比　　她是头纯种的小猎犬，很爱我；怎样？

安 德 鲁　　我也曾经给人爱过呢。

托　　比　　我们去睡吧，骑士。你应该叫家里再寄些钱来。

安 德 鲁　　要是我不能得到你的侄女，我就大上其当了。

托　　比　　去要钱吧，骑士；要是你结果终不能得到她，你就叫我傻子。

安 德 鲁　　要是我不去要，就再不要相信我，随你怎么办。

托　　比　　来，来，我去烫些酒来；现在去睡太晚了。来，骑士；来，骑士。

同下。

SCENE IV

A room in DUKE ORSINO's palace.
Enter DUKE ORSINO, VIOLA, CURIO, and others.

DUKE	Give me some music. Now, good morrow, friends.
	Now, good Cesario, but that piece of song,
	That old and antique song we heard last night:
	Methought it did relieve my passion much,
	More than light airs and recollected terms
	Of these most brisk and giddy-paced times:
	Come, but one verse.
CURIO	He is not here, so please your lo rdship that should sing it.
DUKE	Who was it?
CURIO	Feste, the jester, my lord; a fool that the lady
	Olivia's father took much delight in. He is about the house.
DUKE	Seek him out, and play the tune the while.

Exit CURIO. Music plays.

Come hither, boy: if ever thou shalt love,
In the sweet pangs of it remember me;
For such as I am all true lovers are,
Unstaid and skittish in all motions else,
Save in the constant image of the creature
That is beloved. How dost thou like this tune?

VIOLA	It gives a very echo to the seat
	Where Love is thron'd.
DUKE	Thou dost speak masterly:
	My life upon't, young though thou art, thine eye
	Hath stay'd upon some favour that it loves:
	Hath it not, boy?
VIOLA	A little, by your favour.

第四场

公爵府中一室。

公爵、薇奥拉、丘里奥及余人等上。

公　爵　给我奏些音乐。早安,朋友们。好西萨里奥,我只要听我们昨晚听的那支古曲;我觉得它比目前轻音乐中那种轻情的乐调和警炼的字句更能慰解我的痴情。来,只唱一节吧。

丘里奥　启禀殿下,会唱这歌儿的人不在这儿。

公　爵　他是谁?

丘里奥　是那个弄人费斯特,殿下;他是奥丽维娅小姐的尊翁所宠幸的傻子。他就在这儿左近。

公　爵　去找他来,现在先把那曲调奏起来吧。

丘里奥下。奏乐。

过来,孩子。要是你有一天和人恋爱了,请在甜蜜的痛苦中记着我;因为真心的恋人都像我一样,在其他一切情感上都是轻浮易变,但他所爱的人儿的影像,却永远铭刻在他的心头。你喜不喜欢这个曲调?

薇奥拉　它传出了爱情的宝座上的回声。

公　爵　你说得很好。我相信你虽然这样年轻,你的眼睛一定曾经看中过什么人;是不是,孩子?

薇奥拉　略为有点,请您恕我。

DUKE	What kind of woman is't?
VIOLA	Of your complexion.
DUKE	She is not worth thee, then. What years, i' faith?
VIOLA	About your years, my lord.
DUKE	Too old by heaven: let still the woman take
	An elder than herself: so wears she to him,
	So sways she level in her husband's heart:
	For, boy, however we do praise ourselves,
	Our fancies are more giddy and unfirm,
	More longing, wavering, sooner lost and worn,
	Than women's are.
VIOLA	I think it well, my lord.
DUKE	Then let thy love be younger than thyself,
	Or thy affection cannot hold the bent;
	For women are as roses, whose fair flower
	Being once display'd, doth fall that very hour.
VIOLA	And so they are: alas, that they are so;
	To die, even when they to perfection grow!

Re-enter CURIO and Clown.

DUKE	O, fellow, come, the song we had last night.
	Mark it, Cesario, it is old and plain;
	The spinsters and the knitters in the sun
	And the free maids that weave their thread with bones
	Do use to chant it: it is silly sooth,
	And dallies with the innocence of love,
	Like the old age.
Clown	Are you ready, sir?
DUKE	Ay; prithee, sing.

Music.

公　　爵　　是个什么样子的女人呢？
薇奥拉　　相貌跟您差不多。
公　　爵　　那么她是不配被你爱的。什么年纪呢？
薇奥拉　　年纪也跟您差不多，殿下。
公　　爵　　啊，那太老了！女人应当拣一个比她年纪大些的男人，这样她才跟他合得拢来，不会失去她丈夫的欢心；因为，孩子，不论我们怎样自称自赞，我们的爱情总比女人们流动不定些，富于希求，易于反复，更容易消失而生厌。

薇奥拉　　这一层我也想到，殿下。
公　　爵　　那么选一个比你年轻一点的姑娘做你的爱人吧，否则你的爱情便不能常青——
女人正像是娇艳的蔷薇，
花开才不久便转眼枯萎。
薇奥拉　　是啊，可叹她刹那的光荣，早枝头零落留不住东风！

　　　　　　丘里奥偕小丑重上。

公　　爵　　啊，朋友！来，把我们昨夜听的那支歌儿再唱一遍。好好听着，西萨里奥。那是个古老而平凡的歌儿，是晒着太阳的纺线工人和织布工人以及无忧无虑的制花边的女郎们常唱的；歌里的话儿都是些平常不过的真理，搬弄着纯朴的古代的那种爱情的纯洁。

小　　丑　　您预备好了吗，殿下？
公　　爵　　好，请你唱吧。

　　　　　　奏乐。

Clown	*[SONG].*
	Come away, come away, death,
	And in sad cypress let me be laid;
	Fly away, fly away breath;
	I am slain by a fair cruel maid.
	My shroud of white, stuck all with yew,
	O, prepare it!
	My part of death, no one so true
	Did share it.
	Not a flower, not a flower sweet
	On my black coffin let there be strown;
	Not a friend, not a friend greet
	My poor corpse, where my bones shall be thrown:
	A thousand thousand sighs to save,
	Lay me, O, where
	Sad true lover never find my grave,
	To weep there!
DUKE	There's for thy pains.
Clown	No pains, sir: I take pleasure in singing, sir.
DUKE	I'll pay thy pleasure then.
Clown	Truly, sir, and pleasure will be paid, one time or another.
DUKE	Give me now leave to leave thee.
Clown	Now, the melancholy god protect thee; and the tailor make thy doublet of changeable taffeta, for thy mind is a very opal. I would have men of such constancy put to sea, that their business might be every thing and their intent every where; for that's it that always makes a good voyage of nothing. Farewell.

Exit.

小　丑　（唱）
　　　　　过来吧，过来吧，死神！
　　　　　让我横陈在凄凉的柏棺①的中央；
　　　　　飞去吧，飞去吧，浮生！
　　　　　我被害于一个狠心的美貌姑娘。
　　　　　为我罩上白色的殓衾铺满紫衫；
　　　　　没有一个真心的人为我而悲哀。
　　　　　莫让一朵花儿甜柔，
　　　　　撒上了我那黑色的、黑色的棺材；
　　　　　没有一个朋友迓候
　　　　　我尸身，不久我的骨骼将会散开。
　　　　　免得多情的人们千万次的感伤，
　　　　　请把我埋葬在无从凭吊的荒场。

公　爵　这是赏给你的辛苦钱。
小　丑　一点不辛苦，殿下；我以唱歌为乐呢。
公　爵　那么就算赏给你的快乐钱。
小　丑　不错，殿下，快乐总是要付出代价的。
公　爵　现在允许我不再见你吧。
小　丑　好，忧愁之神保佑着你！但愿裁缝用闪缎给你裁一身衫子，因为你的心就像猫眼石那样闪烁不定。我希望像这种没有恒心的人都航海去，好让他们过着五湖四海，千变万化的生活；因为这样的人总会两手空空地回家。再会。

　　　　　　　　　　　下。

---

① 此处"柏棺"原文为Cypress，自来注家均肯定应作Crape(丧礼用之黑色绉纱)解释；按字面解Cypress为一种杉柏之属，径译"柏棺"在语调上似乎更为适当，故仍将错就错，据字面译。

DUKE Let all the rest give place.

CURIO and Attendants retire.

Once more, Cesario,
Get thee to yond same sovereign cruelty:
Tell her, my love, more noble than the world,
Prizes not quantity of dirty lands;
The parts that fortune hath bestow'd upon her,
Tell her, I hold as giddily as fortune;
But 'tis that miracle and queen of gems
That nature pranks her in attracts my soul.

VIOLA But if she cannot love you, sir?

DUKE I cannot be so answer'd.

VIOLA Sooth, but you must.
Say that some lady, as perhaps there is,
Hath for your love a great a pang of heart
As you have for Olivia: you cannot love her;
You tell her so; must she not then be answer'd?

DUKE There is no woman's sides
Can bide the beating of so strong a passion
As love doth give my heart; no woman's heart
So big, to hold so much; they lack retention
Alas, their love may be call'd appetite,
No motion of the liver, but the palate,
That suffer surfeit, cloyment and revolt;
But mine is all as hungry as the sea,
And can digest as much: make no compare
Between that love a woman can bear me
And that I owe Olivia.

VIOLA Ay, but I know—

DUKE What dost thou know?

公　爵　　　大家都退开去。

　　　　　　　　　　　丘里奥及侍从等下。

西萨里奥，你再给我到那位狠心的女王那边去；对她说，我的爱情是超越世间的，泥污的土地不是我所看重的事物；命运所赐给她的尊荣财富，你对她说，在我的眼中都像命运一样无常；吸引我的灵魂的是她的天赋的灵奇，绝世的仙姿。

薇奥拉　　可是假如她不能爱您呢，殿下？
公　爵　　我不能得到这样的回音。
薇奥拉　　可是您不能不得到这样的回音。假如有一位姑娘——也许真有那么一个人——也像您爱着奥丽维娅一样痛苦地爱着您；您不能爱她，您这样告诉她；那么她岂不是必得以这样的答复为满足吗？

公　爵　　女人的小小的身体一定受不住像爱情强加于我心中的那种激烈的搏跳；女人的心没有这样广大，可以藏得下这许多；她们缺少含忍的能力。唉，她们的爱就像一个人的口味一样，不是从脏腑里，而是从舌尖上感觉到的，过饱了便会食伤呕吐；可是我的爱就像饥饿的大海，能够消化一切。不要把一个女人所能对我发生的爱情跟我对于奥丽维娅的爱情相提并论吧。

薇奥拉　　哦，可是我知道——
公　爵　　你知道什么？

VIOLA	Too well what love women to men may owe:
	In faith, they are as true of heart as we.
	My father had a daughter loved a man,
	As it might be, perhaps, were I a woman,
	I should your lordship.
DUKE	And what's her history?
VIOLA	A blank, my lord. She never told her love,
	But let concealment, like a worm i' the bud,
	Feed on her damask cheek: she pined in thought,
	And with a green and yellow melancholy
	She sat like patience on a monument,
	Smiling at grief. Was not this love indeed?
	We men may say more, swear more: but indeed
	Our shows are more than will; for still we prove
	Much in our vows, but little in our love.
DUKE	But died thy sister of her love, my boy?
VIOLA	I am all the daughters of my father's house,
	And all the brothers too: and yet I know not.
	Sir, shall I to this lady?
DUKE	Ay, that's the theme.
	To her in haste; give her this jewel; say,
	My love can give no place, bide no denay.

Exeunt.

| 薇奥拉 | 我知道得很清楚女人对于男人会怀着怎样的爱情；真的，她们是跟我们一样真心的。我的父亲有一个女儿，她爱上了一个男人，正像假如我是个女人也许会爱上了您殿下一样。 |

| 公　爵 | 她的历史怎样？ |
| 薇奥拉 | 一片空白而已，殿下。她从来不向人诉说她的爱情，让隐藏在内心中的抑郁像蓓蕾中的蛀虫一样，侵蚀着她的绯红的脸颊；她因相思而憔悴，疾病和忧愁折磨着她，像是墓碑上刻着的"忍耐"的化身，默坐着向悲哀微笑。这不是真的爱情吗？我们男人也许更多话，更会发誓，可是我们所表示的，总多于我们所决心实行的；不论我们怎样山盟海誓，我们的爱情总不过如此。 |

| 公　爵 | 但是你的姊姊有没有殉情而死，我的孩子？ |
| 薇奥拉 | 我父亲的女儿只有我一个，儿子也只有我一个——可她有没有殉情我不知道。殿下，我要不要就去见这位小姐？ |

| 公　爵 | 对了，这是正事——
快前去，送给她这颗珍珠；
说我的爱情永不会认输。 |

各下。

SCENE V

OLIVIA's garden.
Enter SIR TOBY BELCH, SIR ANDREW AGUECHEEK and FABIAN.

SIR TOBY Come thy ways, Signior Fabian.

FABIAN Nay, I'll come: if I lose a scruple of this sport, let me be boiled to death with melancholy.

SIR TOBY Wouldst thou not be glad to have the niggardly rascally sheep-biter come by some notable shame?

FABIAN I would exult, man: you know, he brought me out o' favour with my lady about a bear-baiting here.

SIR TOBY To anger him we'll have the bear again; and we will fool him black and blue: shall we not, Sir Andrew?

SIR ANDREW An we do not, it is pity of our lives.

SIR TOBY Here comes the little villain.

Enter MARIA.

SIR TOBY How now, my metal of India!

MARIA Get ye all three into the box-tree: Malvolio's coming down this walk: he has been yonder i' the sun practising behavior to his own shadow this half hour: observe him, for the love of mockery; for I know this letter will make a contemplative idiot of him. Close, in the name of jesting! Lie thou there, *[Throws down a letter]* for here comes the trout that must be caught with tickling.

Exit.
Enter MALVOLIO.

MALVOLIO 'Tis but fortune; all is fortune. Maria once told me she did affect me: and I have heard herself come thus near, that, should she fancy, it should be one of my complexion.

第五场

奥丽维娅的花园。
托比·培尔契爵士、安德鲁·艾古契克爵士及费边上。

托　比　　来吧，费边先生。
费　边　　噢，我就来；要是我把这场好戏略为错过了一点点儿，让我在懊恼里煎死了吧。
托　比　　让这个卑鄙龌龊的丑东西出一场丑，你高兴不高兴？
费　边　　我才要快活死哩！您知道那次我因为耍熊，被他在小姐跟前说我坏话。
托　比　　我们再把那头熊牵来激他发怒；我们要把他作弄得体无完肤。你说怎样，安德鲁爵士？
安　德　鲁　要是我们不那么做，那才是终身的憾事呢。
托　比　　小坏东西来了。

玛利娅上。

托　比　　啊，我的小宝贝！
玛利娅　　你们三人都躲到黄杨树后面去。马伏里奥正从这条道上走过来了；他已经在那边太阳光底下对他自己的影子练习了半个钟头仪法。谁要是喜欢笑话，就留心瞧着他吧；我知道这封信一定会叫他变成一个发痴的呆子的。凭着玩笑的名义，躲起来吧！你躺在那边；（丢下一信）这条鲟鱼已经来了，你不去撩撩他的痒处是捉不到手的。

下。
马伏里奥上。

马伏里奥　不过是运气；一切都是运气。玛利娅曾经对我说过小姐喜欢我；我也曾经听见她自己说过那样的话，说要是她爱上了人的话，一定要选像我这种脾气的人。而且，她待我比待其他的下人显得分

| | Besides, she uses me with a more exalted respect than any one else that follows her.
What should I think on't? |
|---|---|
| SIR TOBY | Here's an overweening rogue! |
| FABIAN | O, peace! Contemplation makes a rare turkey-cock of him: how he jets under his advanced plumes! |
| SIR ANDREW | 'Slight, I could so beat the rogue! |
| SIR TOBY | Peace, I say. |
| MALVOLIO | To be Count Malvolio! |
| SIR TOBY | Ah, rogue! |
| SIR ANDREW | Pistol him, pistol him. |
| SIR TOBY | Peace, peace! |
| MALVOLIO | There is example for't; the lady of the Strachy married the yeoman of the wardrobe. |
| SIR ANDREW | Fie on him, Jezebel! |
| FABIAN | O, peace! now he's deeply in: look how imagination blows him. |
| MALVOLIO | Having been three months married to her, sitting in my state,— |
| SIR TOBY | O, for a stone-bow, to hit him in the eye! |
| MALVOLIO | Calling my officers about me, in my branched velvet gown; having come from a day-bed, where I have left Olivia sleeping,— |
| SIR TOBY | Fire and brimstone! |
| FABIAN | O, peace, peace! |
| MALVOLIO | And then to have the humour of state; and after a demure travel of regard, telling them I know my place as I would they should do theirs, to for my kinsman Toby,— |
| SIR TOBY | Bolts and shackles! |
| FABIAN | O peace, peace, peace! now, now. |
| MALVOLIO | Seven of my people, with an obedient start, make out for |

外尊敬。这点我应该怎么解释呢?

托　　比　　瞧这个自命不凡的混蛋!
费　　边　　静些!他已经痴心妄想得变成一头出色的火鸡了;瞧他那种蓬起了羽毛高视阔步的样子!
安 德 鲁　　他妈的,我可以把这混蛋痛打一顿!
托　　比　　别闹啦!
马伏里奥　　做了马伏里奥伯爵!
托　　比　　啊,混蛋!
安 德 鲁　　给他吃手枪!给他吃手枪!
托　　比　　别闹!别闹!
马伏里奥　　这种事情是有前例可援的;斯特拉契夫人也下嫁给家臣。

安 德 鲁　　该死,这畜生!
费　　边　　静些!现在他着了魔啦;瞧他越想越得意。

马伏里奥　　跟她结婚过了三个月,我坐在我的宝座上——

托　　比　　啊!我要弹一颗石子到他的眼睛里去!
马伏里奥　　身上披着绣花的丝绒袍子,召唤我的臣僚过来;那时我刚睡罢午觉,撇下奥丽维娅酣睡未醒——

托　　比　　大火硫磺烧死他!
费　　边　　静些!静些!
马伏里奥　　那时我装出一副威严的神气,先目光凛凛地向众人瞜视一周,对他们表示我知道我的地位,他们也必须明白自己的身份;然后吩咐他们去请我的托比老叔过来——
托　　比　　把他铐起来!
费　　边　　别闹!别闹!别闹!好啦!好啦!
马伏里奥　　我的七个仆人恭恭敬敬地前去找他。我皱了皱眉头,或者给我的

	him: I frown the while; and perchance wind up watch, or play with my—some rich jewel. Toby approaches; courtesies there to me,—
SIR TOBY	Shall this fellow live?
FABIAN	Though our silence be drawn from us with cars, yet peace.
MALVOLIO	I extend my hand to him thus, quenching my familiar smile with an austere regard of control,—
SIR TOBY	And does not Toby take you a blow o' the lips then?
MALVOLIO	Saying, 'Cousin Toby, my fortunes having cast me on your niece give me this prerogative of speech,'—
SIR TOBY	What, what?
MALVOLIO	'You must amend your drunkenness.'
SIR TOBY	Out, scab!
FABIAN	Nay, patience, or we break the sinews of our plot.
MALVOLIO	'Besides, you waste the treasure of your time with a foolish knight,'—
SIR ANDREW	That's me, I warrant you.
MALVOLIO	'One Sir Andrew,'—
SIR ANDREW	I knew 'twas I; for many do call me fool.
MALVOLIO	What employment have we here?

Taking up the letter.

FABIAN	Now is the woodcock near the gin.
SIR TOBY	O, peace! and the spirit of humour intimate reading aloud to him!
MALVOLIO	By my life, this is my lady's hand these be her very C's, her U's and her T's and thus makes she her great P's. It is, in contempt of question, her hand.
SIR ANDREW	Her C's, her U's and her T's: why that?
MALVOLIO	*[Reads]* 'To the unknown beloved, this, and my good wishes:'— her very phrases! By your leave, wax.

表上了上弦，或者抚弄着我的——什么珠宝之类。托比来了，向我行了个礼——

托　　比	这家伙可以让他活命吗？
费　　边	哪怕有几辆马车要把我们的静默拉走，也不要闹吧！
马伏里奥	我这样向他伸出手去，用一副庄严的威势来抑住我的亲昵的笑容——
托　　比	那时托比不就给了你一个嘴巴子吗？
马伏里奥	说，"托比叔父，我已蒙令侄女不弃下嫁，请您准许我这样说话——"
托　　比	什么？什么？
马伏里奥	"你必须把喝酒的习惯戒掉。"
托　　比	他妈的，这狗东西！
费　　边	哎，别生气，否则我们的计策就要失败了。
马伏里奥	"而且，您还把您的宝贵的光阴跟一个傻瓜骑士在一块儿浪费——"
安 德 鲁	说的是我，一定的啦。
马伏里奥	"那个安德鲁爵士——"
安 德 鲁	我知道是我；因为许多人都管我叫傻瓜。
马伏里奥	这儿有些什么东西呢？

见信。

费　　边	现在那蠢鸟走近陷阱旁边来了。
托　　比	啊，静些！但愿能操纵人心意的神灵叫他高声朗读。
马伏里奥	（拾信）哎哟，这是小姐的手笔！瞧这一钩一弯一横一直那不正是她的笔锋吗？没有问题，一定是她写的。
安 德 鲁	她的一钩一弯一横一直，那是什么意思？
马伏里奥	（读）"给不知名的恋人，至诚的祝福。"完全是她的口气！对不住，封蜡。且慢！这封口上的钤记不就是她一直用作封印的鲁

	Soft! and the impressure her Lucrece, with which she uses to seal: 'tis my lady. To whom should this be?
FABIAN	This wins him, liver and all.
MALVOLIO	*[Reads]*
	Jove knows I love: But who?
	Lips, do not move;
	No man must know.
	'No man must know.' What follows? the numbers altered!
	'No man must know:' if this should be thee, Malvolio?
SIR TOBY	Marry, hang thee, brock!
MALVOLIO	*[Reads]*
	I may command where I adore;
	But silence, like a Lucrece knife,
	With bloodless stroke my heart doth gore:
	M, O, A, I, doth sway my life.
FABIAN	A fustian riddle!
SIR TOBY	Excellent wench, say I.
MALVOLIO	'M, O, A, I, doth sway my life.' Nay, but first, let me see, let me see, let me see.
FABIAN	What dish o' poison has she dressed him!
SIR TOBY	And with what wing the staniel cheques at it!
MALVOLIO	'I may command where I adore.' Why, she may command me: I serve her; she is my lady. Why, this is evident to any formal capacity; there is no obstruction in this: and the end,—what should that alphabetical position portend? If I could make that resemble something in me,—Softly! M, O, A, I,—
SIR TOBY	O, ay, make up that: he is now at a cold scent.
FABIAN	Sowter will cry upon't for all this, though it be as rank as a fox.
MALVOLIO	M,—Malvolio; M,—why, that begins my name.

克丽丝的肖像吗？一定是我的小姐。可是那是写给谁的呢？

费　　边　　这叫他心窝儿里都痒起来了。
马伏里奥　　（读）

知我者天，
我爱为谁？
慎莫多言，
莫令人知。

"莫令人知。"下面还写些什么？又换了句调了！"莫令人知"：说的也许是你哩，马伏里奥！

托　　比　　嘿，该死，这獾子！
马伏里奥　　（读）

我可以向我所爱的人发号施令；
但隐秘的衷情如鲁克丽丝之刀，
杀人不见血地把我的深心割刃：
我的命在M，O，A，I的手里飘摇。

费　　边　　无聊的谜语！
托　　比　　我说是个好丫头。
马伏里奥　　"我的命在M，O，A，I的手里飘摇。"不，让我先想一想，让我想一想，让我想一想。
费　　边　　她给他吃了一服多好的毒药！
托　　比　　瞧那头鹰儿多么饿急似的想一口吞下去！
马伏里奥　　"我可以向我所爱的人发号施令。"哦，她可以命令我；我侍候着她，她是我的小姐。这是无论哪个有一点点脑子的人都看得出来的；全然合得拢。可是那结尾一句，那几个字母又是什么意思呢？能不能牵附到我的身上？——慢慢！M，O，A，I——

托　　比　　哎，这应该想个法儿；他弄糊涂了。
费　　边　　即使像一头狐狸那样臊气冲天，这狗子也会闻出味来，汪汪地叫起来的。
马伏里奥　　M，马伏里奥；M，嘿，那正是我的名字的第一个字母哩。

FABIAN	Did not I say he would work it out? the cur is excellent at faults.
MALVOLIO	M,—but then there is no consonancy in the sequel; that suffers under probation A should follow but O does.
FABIAN	And O shall end, I hope.
SIR TOBY	Ay, or I'll cudgel him, and make him cry O!
MALVOLIO	And then I comes behind.
FABIAN	Ay, an you had any eye behind you, you might see more detraction at your heels than fortunes before you.
MALVOLIO	M, O, A, I; this simulation is not as the former: and yet, to crush this a little, it would bow to me, for every one of these letters are in my name. Soft! here follows prose.

Reads.

'If this fall into thy hand, revolve. In my stars I am above thee; but be not afraid of greatness: some are born great, some achieve greatness, and some have greatness thrust upon 'em. Thy Fates open their hands; let thy blood and spirit embrace them; and, to inure thyself to what thou art like to be, cast thy humble slough and appear fresh. Be opposite with a kinsman, surly with servants; let thy tongue tang arguments of state; put thyself into the trick of singularity: she thus advises thee that sighs for thee. Remember who commended thy yellow stockings, and wished to see thee ever cross-gartered: I say, remember. Go to, thou art made, if thou desirest to be so; if not, let me see thee a steward still, the fellow of servants, and not worthy to touch Fortune's fingers. Farewell.
She that would alter services with thee,
The fortunate-unhappy.'

费　边	我不是说他会想出来的吗？这狗的鼻子在没有味的地方也会闻出味来。
马伏里奥	M——可是这次序不大对；这样一试，反而不成功了。跟着来的应该是个A字，可是却是个O字。
费　边	我希望O字应该放在结尾的吧？
托　比	对了，否则我要揍他一顿，让他喊出个"O！"来。
马伏里奥	A的背后又跟着个I。
费　边	哼，要是你背后生眼睛①的话，你就知道你眼前并没有什么幸运，你的背后却有倒霉的事跟着呢。
马伏里奥	M，O，A，I；这隐语可跟前面所说的不很合辙；可是稍为把它颠倒一下，也就可以适合我了，因为这几个字母都在我的名字里。且慢！这儿还有散文呢。

读。

"要是这封信落到你手里，请你想一想。照我的命运而论，我是在你之上，可是你不用惧怕富贵：有的人是生来的富贵，有的人是挣来的富贵，有的人是送上来的富贵。你的好运已经向你伸出手来，赶快用你的全副精神抱住它。你应该练习一下怎样才合乎你所将要做的那种人的身份，脱去你卑恭的旧习，放出一些活泼的神气来。对亲戚不妨分庭抗礼，对仆人不妨摆摆架子；你嘴里要鼓唇弄舌地谈些国家大事，装出一副矜持的样子。为你叹息的人儿这样吩咐着你。记着谁曾经赞美过你的黄袜子，愿意看见你永远扎着十字交叉的袜带；我对你说，你记着吧。好，只要你自己愿意，你就可以出头了；否则让我见你一生一世做个管家，与众仆为伍，不值得抬举。再会！我是愿意跟你交换地位的，幸运的不幸者。"

---

① 眼睛原文为eye，音与I音相近。

Daylight and champaign discovers not more: this is open. I will be proud, I will read politic authors, I will baffle Sir Toby, I will wash off gross acquaintance, I will be point-devise the very man. I do not now fool myself, to let imagination jade me; for every reason excites to this, that my lady loves me. She did commend my yellow stockings of late, she did praise my leg being cross-gartered; and in this she manifests herself to my love, and with a kind of injunction drives me to these habits of her liking. I thank my stars I am happy. I will be strange, stout, in yellow stockings, and cross-gartered, even with the swiftness of putting on. Jove and my stars be praised! Here is yet a postscript.

Reads.

'Thou canst not choose but know who I am. If thou entertainest my love, let it appear in thy smiling; thy smiles become thee well; therefore in my presence still smile, dear my sweet, I prithee.'

Jove, I thank thee: I will smile; I will do everything that thou wilt have me.

Exit.

FABIAN	I will not give my part of this sport for a pension of thousands to be paid from the Sophy.
SIR TOBY	I could marry this wench for this device.
SIR ANDREW	So could I too.
SIR TOBY	And ask no other dowry with her but such another jest.
SIR ANDREW	Nor I neither.
FABIAN	Here comes my noble gull-catcher.

Re-enter MARIA.

青天白日也没有这么明白，平原旷野也没有这么显豁。我要摆起架子来，谈起国家大事来；我要叫托比丧气，我要断绝那些鄙贱之交，我要一点不含糊地做起这么一个人来。我没有自己哄骗自己，让想象把我愚弄；因为每一个理由都指点着说，我的小姐爱上了我了。她最近称赞过我的黄袜子和我的十字交叉的袜带；她就是用这方法表示她爱我，用一种命令的方法叫我打扮成她所喜欢的样式。谢谢我的命星，我好幸福！我要放出高傲的神气来，穿了黄袜子，扎着十字交叉的袜带，立刻就去装束起来。赞美上帝和我的命星！这儿还有附启：

读。

"你一定想得到我是谁。要是你接受我的爱情，请你用微笑表示你的意思；你的微笑是很好看的。我的好人儿，请你当着我的面前永远微笑着吧。"

上帝，我谢谢你！我要微笑；我要做每一件你吩咐我做的事。

下。

费　边	即使波斯王给我一笔几千块钱的恩俸，我也不愿错过这场玩意儿。
托　比	这丫头想得出这种主意，我简直可以娶了她。
安德鲁	我也可以娶了她呢。
托　比	我不要她什么妆奁，只要再给我想出这么一个笑话来就行了。
安德鲁	我也不要她什么妆奁。
费　边	我那位捉蠢鹅的好手来了。

玛利娅重上。

SIR TOBY Wilt thou set thy foot o' my neck?

SIR ANDREW Or o' mine either?

SIR TOBY Shall I play my freedom at tray-trip, and become thy bond-slave?

SIR ANDREW I' faith, or I either?

SIR TOBY Why, thou hast put him in such a dream, that when the image of it leaves him he must run mad.

MARIA Nay, but say true; does it work upon him?

SIR TOBY Like aqua-vitae with a midwife.

MARIA If you will then see the fruits of the sport, mark his first approach before my lady: he will come to her in yellow stockings, and 'tis a colour she abhors, and cross-gartered, a fashion she detests; and he will smile upon her, which will now be so unsuitable to her disposition, being addicted to a melancholy as she is, that it cannot but turn him into a notable contempt. If you will see it, follow me.

SIR TOBY To the gates of Tartar, thou most excellent devil of wit!

SIR ANDREW I'll make one too.

Exeunt.

托　　比	你愿意把你的脚搁在我的头颈上吗？
安 德 鲁	或者搁在我的头颈上？
托　　比	要不要我把我的自由作孤注一掷，做你的奴隶？

安 德 鲁	是的，要不要我也做你的奴隶？
托　　比	你已经叫他大做其梦，要是那种幻象一离开了他，他一定会发疯的。

玛 利 娅	可是您老实对我说，他中计了吗？
托　　比	就像收生婆喝了烧酒一样。
玛 利 娅	要是你们要看看这场把戏会闹出些什么结果来，请看好他怎样到小姐跟前去：他会穿起了黄袜子，那正是她所讨厌的颜色；还要扎着十字交叉的袜带，那正是她所厌恶的式样；他还要向她微笑，照她现在那样悒郁的心境，她一定会不高兴，管保叫他大受一场没趣。假如你们要看的话，跟我来吧。

托　　比	好，就是到地狱门口也行，你这好机灵鬼！
安 德 鲁	我也要去。

同下。

ACT Ⅲ 第三幕

SCENE I

OLIVIA's garden.

Enter VIOLA, and Clown with a tabour.

VIOLA Save thee, friend, and thy music: Dost thou live by thy tabour?

Clown No, sir, I live by the church.

VIOLA Art thou a churchman?

Clown No such matter, sir: I do live by the church; for I do live at my house, and my house doth stand by the church.

VIOLA So thou mayst say, the king lies by a beggar, if a beggar dwell near him; or, the church stands by thy tabour, if thy tabour stand by the church.

Clown You have said, sir. To see this age! A sentence is but a cheveril glove to a good wit: how quickly the wrong side may be turned outward!

VIOLA Nay, that's certain; they that dally nicely with words may quickly make them wanton.

Clown I would, therefore, my sister had had no name, sir.

VIOLA Why, man?

Clown Why, sir, her name's a word; and to dally with that word might make my sister wanton. But indeed words are very rascals since bonds disgraced them.

VIOLA Thy reason, man?

Clown Troth, sir, I can yield you none without words; and words are grown so false, I am loath to prove reason with them.

VIOLA I warrant thou art a merry fellow and carest for nothing.

Clown Not so, sir, I do care for something; but in my conscience, sir, I do not care for you: if that be to care for nothing, sir, I would it would make you invisible.

VIOLA Art not thou the Lady Olivia's fool?

Clown No, indeed, sir; the Lady Olivia has no folly: she will

第一场

奥丽维娅的花园。
薇奥拉及小丑持手鼓上。

薇奥拉　上帝保佑你和你的音乐,朋友!你是靠着打手鼓过日子的吗?

小　丑　不,先生,我靠着教堂过日子。

薇奥拉　你是个教士吗?

小　丑　没有的事,先生。我靠着教堂过日子,因为我住在我的家里,而我的家是在教堂附近。

薇奥拉　你也可以说,国王住在叫花窝的附近,因为叫花子住在王宫的附近;教堂筑在你的手鼓旁边,因为你的手鼓放在教堂旁边。

小　丑　您说得对,先生。人们一代比一代聪明了!一句话对于一个聪明人就像是一副小山羊皮的手套,一下子就可以翻了转来。

薇奥拉　嗯,那是一定的啦;善于在字面上翻弄花样的,很容易流于轻薄。

小　丑　那么,先生,我希望我的妹妹不要有名字。

薇奥拉　为什么呢,朋友?

小　丑　先生,她的名字不也是个字吗?在那个字上面翻弄翻弄花样,也许我的妹妹就会轻薄起来。可是文字自从失去自由以后,也就变成很危险的家伙了。

薇奥拉　你说出理由来,朋友?

小　丑　不瞒您说,先生,要是我向您说出理由来,那非得用文字不可;可是现在文字变得那么坏,我真不高兴用它们来证明我的理由。

薇奥拉　我敢说你是个快活的家伙,万事都不关心。

小　丑　不是的,先生,我所关心的事倒有一点儿;可是凭良心说,先生,我可一点不关心您;如果不关心您就是无所关心的话,先生,我倒希望您也能够化为乌有才好。

薇奥拉　你不是奥丽维娅小姐府中的傻子吗?

小　丑　真的不是,先生。奥丽维娅小姐不喜欢傻气;她要嫁了人才会在

	keep no fool, sir, till she be married; and fools are as like husbands as pilchards are to herrings; the husband's the bigger: I am indeed not her fool, but her corrupter of words.
VIOLA	I saw thee late at the Count Orsino's.
Clown	Foolery, sir, does walk about the orb like the sun, it shines every where. I would be sorry, sir, but the fool should be as oft with your master as with my mistress: I think I saw your wisdom there.
VIOLA	Nay, an thou pass upon me, I'll no more with thee. Hold, there's expenses for thee.

She gives him a coin.

Clown	Now Jove, in his next commodity of hair, send thee a beard!
VIOLA	By my troth, I'll tell thee, I am almost sick for one; Aside though I would not have it grow on my chin. Is thy lady within?
Clown	*[Still gazes at the coin]* Would not a pair of these have bred, sir?
VIOLA	Yes, being kept together and put to use.
Clown	I would play Lord Pandarus of Phrygia, sir, to bring a Cressida to this Troilus.
VIOLA	I understand you, sir; 'tis well begged.
Clown	The matter, I hope, is not great, sir, begging but a beggar: Cressida was a beggar. My lady is within, sir. I will construe to them whence you come; who you are and what you would are out of my welkin, I might say 'element,' but the word is over-worn.

Exit.

	家里养起傻子来，先生；傻子之于丈夫，犹之乎小鱼之于大鱼，丈夫不过是个大一点的傻子而已。我真的不是她的傻子，我是给她说说笑话的人。
薇奥拉	我最近曾经在奥西诺公爵的地方看见过你。
小　丑	先生，傻气就像太阳一样环绕着地球，到处放射它的光辉。要是傻子不常到您主人那里去，如同常在我的小姐那儿一样，那么，先生，我可真是抱歉。我想我也曾经在那边看见过您这聪明人。
薇奥拉	哼，你要在我身上打趣，我可要不睬你了。拿去，这个钱给你。

给他一枚钱币。

小　丑	好，上帝保佑您长起胡子来吧！
薇奥拉	老实告诉你，我倒真为了胡子害相思呢；虽然我不要在自己脸上长起来。小姐在里面吗？
小　丑	（指着钱币）先生，您要是再赏我一个钱，凑成两个，不就可以养儿子了吗？
薇奥拉	不错，如果你拿它们去放债取利息。
小　丑	先生，我愿意做个弗里吉亚的潘达洛斯，给这个特洛伊罗斯找一个克瑞西达来。①
薇奥拉	我知道了，朋友；你很善于乞讨。
小　丑	我希望您不会认为这是非分的乞讨，先生，我要乞讨的不过是个叫花子——克瑞西达后来不是变成个叫花子了吗？小姐就在里面，先生。我可以对他们说明您是从哪儿来的；至于您是谁，您来有什么事，那就不属于我的领域之内了——我应当说"范围"，可是那两个字已经给人用得太熟了。

下。

---

① 关于特洛伊罗斯(Troilus)与克瑞西达(Cressida)恋爱的故事可参看莎士比亚所著悲剧《特洛伊罗斯与克瑞西达》。潘达洛斯(Pandarus)系克瑞西达之舅，为他们居间撮合者。克瑞西达因生性轻浮，后被人所弃，沦为乞丐。

VIOLA	This fellow is wise enough to play the fool;
	And to do that well craves a kind of wit:
	He must observe their mood on whom he jests,
	The quality of persons, and the time,
	And, like the haggard, cheque at every feather
	That comes before his eye. This is a practise
	As full of labour as a wise man's art
	For folly that he wisely shows is fit;
	But wise men, folly-fall'n, quite taint their wit.

Enter SIR TOBY BELCH, and SIR ANDREW.

SIR TOBY	Save you, gentleman.
VIOLA	And you, sir.
SIR ANDREW	Dieu vous garde, monsieur.
VIOLA	Et vous aussi; votre serviteur.
SIR ANDREW	I hope, sir, you are; and I am yours.
SIR TOBY	Will you encounter the house? my niece is desirous you should enter, if your trade be to her.
VIOLA	I am bound to your niece, sir; I mean, she is the list of my voyage.
SIR TOBY	Taste your legs, sir; put them to motion.
VIOLA	My legs do better understand me, sir, than I understand what you mean by bidding me taste my legs.
SIR TOBY	I mean, to go, sir, to enter.
VIOLA	I will answer you with gait and entrance. But we are prevented.

Enter OLIVIA and MARIA.

Most excellent accomplished lady, the heavens rain odours on you!

| 薇奥拉 | 这家伙扮傻子很有点儿聪明。装傻装得好也是要靠才情的：他必须窥伺被他所取笑的人们的心情，了解他们的身份，还得看准了时机；然后像窥伺着眼前每一只鸟雀的野鹰一样，每个机会都不放松。这是一种和聪明人的艺术一样艰难的工作：傻子不妨说几句聪明话，聪明人说傻话难免笑骂。|

托比·培尔契爵士、安德鲁·艾古契克爵士同上。

托 比	您好，先生。
薇奥拉	您好，爵士。
安德鲁	上帝保佑您，先生。
薇奥拉	上帝保佑您，我是您的仆人。
安德鲁	先生，我希望您是我的仆人；我也是您的仆人。

| 托 比 | 请您进去吧。舍侄女有请，要是您是来看她的话。|
| 薇奥拉 | 我来正是要拜见令侄女，爵士；她是我此行的目标。|

托 比	请您试试您的腿吧，先生；把它们移动起来。
薇奥拉	我的腿倒是听我使唤，爵士，可是我却听不懂您叫我试试我的腿是什么意思？
托 比	我的意思是，先生，请您走，请您进去。
薇奥拉	好，我就移步前进。可是人家已经先来了。

奥丽维娅及玛利娅上。

最卓越最完美的小姐，愿诸天为您散下芬芳的香雾！

SIR ANDREW That youth's a rare courtier: 'Rain odours;' well.

VIOLA My matter hath no voice, to your own most pregnant and vouchsafed ear.

SIR ANDREW 'Odours,' 'pregnant' and 'vouchsafed:' I'll get 'em all three all ready.

OLIVIA Let the garden door be shut, and leave me to my hearing.

Exeunt SIR TOBY BELCH, SIR ANDREW, and MARIA.

Give me your hand, sir.

VIOLA My duty, madam, and most humble service.

OLIVIA What is your name?

VIOLA Cesario is your servant's name, fair princess.

OLIVIA My servant, sir! 'Twas never merry world
Since lowly feigning was call'd compliment:
You're servant to the Count Orsino, youth.

VIOLA And he is yours, and his must needs be yours:
Your servant's servant is your servant, madam.

OLIVIA For him, I think not on him: for his thoughts,
Would they were blanks, rather than fill'd with me!

VIOLA Madam, I come to whet your gentle thoughts On his behalf.

OLIVIA O, by your leave, I pray you,
I bade you never speak again of him:
But, would you undertake another suit,
I had rather hear you to solicit that
Than music from the spheres.

VIOLA Dear lady,—

OLIVIA Give me leave, beseech you. I did send,
After the last enchantment you did here,
A ring in chase of you: so did I abuse
Myself, my servant and, I fear me, you:

安德鲁	那年轻人是一个出色的廷臣。"散下芬芳的香雾"！好得很。
薇奥拉	我的来意，小姐，只能让您自己的玉耳眷听。
安德鲁	"香雾""玉耳""眷听"，我已经学会了三句话了。
奥丽维娅	关上园门，让我们两人谈话。

托比、安德鲁、玛利娅同下。

	把你的手给我，先生。
薇奥拉	小姐，我愿意奉献我的绵薄之力为您效劳。
奥丽维娅	你叫什么名字？
薇奥拉	您仆人的名字是西萨里奥，美貌的公主。
奥丽维娅	我的仆人，先生！自从假作卑恭认为是一种恭维之后，世界上从此不曾有过乐趣。你是奥西诺公爵的仆人，年轻人。
薇奥拉	他是您的仆人，他的仆人自然也是您的仆人；您的仆人的仆人便是您的仆人，小姐。
奥丽维娅	我不高兴想他；我希望他心里空无所有，不要充满着我。
薇奥拉	小姐，我来是要替他说动您那颗温柔的心。
奥丽维娅	啊！对不起，请你不要再提起他了。可是如果你肯为另外一个人求爱，我愿意听你的请求，胜过于听天乐。
薇奥拉	亲爱的小姐——
奥丽维娅	对不起，让我说句话。上次你到这儿来把我迷醉了之后，我叫人拿了个戒指追你；我欺骗了我自己，欺骗了我的仆人，也许欺骗了你；我用那种无耻的狡狯把你明知道不属于你的东西强纳在你手里，一定会使你看不起我。你会怎样想呢？你不曾把我的名誉

	Under your hard construction must I sit,
	To force that on you, in a shameful cunning,
	Which you knew none of yours: what might you think?
	Have you not set mine honour at the stake
	And baited it with all the unmuzzled thoughts
	That tyrannous heart can think? To one of your receiving
	Enough is shown: a cypress, not a bosom,
	Hideth my heart. So, let me hear you speak.
VIOLA	I pity you.
OLIVIA	That's a degree to love.
VIOLA	No, not a grize; for 'tis a vulgar proof,
	That very oft we pity enemies.
OLIVIA	Why, then, methinks 'tis time to smile again.
	O, world, how apt the poor are to be proud!
	If one should be a prey, how much the better
	To fall before the lion than the wolf!

Clock strikes.

	The clock upbraids me with the waste of time.
	Be not afraid, good youth, I will not have you:
	And yet, when wit and youth is come to harvest,
	Your wife is alike to reap a proper man:
	There lies your way, due west.
VIOLA	Then westward-ho! Grace and good disposition
	Attend your ladyship!
	You'll nothing, madam, to my lord by me?
OLIVIA	Stay:
	I prithee, tell me what thou think'st of me.
VIOLA	That you do think you are not what you are.
OLIVIA	If I think so, I think the same of you.
VIOLA	Then think you right: I am not what I am.

拴在桩柱上,让你那残酷的心所想得到的一切思想恣意地把它虐弄吧?像你这样敏慧的人,我已经表示得太露骨了;掩藏着我的心事的,只是一层薄薄的蝉纱。所以,让我听你的意见吧。

薇奥拉　　我可怜你。
奥丽维娅　　那是到达恋爱的一个阶段。
薇奥拉　　不,此路不通,我们对敌人也往往会发生怜悯,这是常有的经验。
奥丽维娅　　啊,听了你的话,我倒是又要笑起来了。世界啊!微贱的人多么容易骄傲!要是做了俘虏,那么落于狮子的爪下比之豺狼的吻中要幸运多少啊!

　　　　　　　　　　　　钟鸣。

时钟在谴责我把时间浪费。别担心,好孩子,我不会留住你。可是等到才情和青春成熟之后,你的妻子将会收获到一个出色的男人。向西是你的路。

薇奥拉　　那么向西开步走!愿小姐称心如意!您没有什么话要我向我的主人说吗,小姐?

奥丽维娅　　且慢,请你告诉我你以为我这人怎样?

薇奥拉　　我以为你以为你不是你自己。
奥丽维娅　　要是我以为这样,我以为你也是这样。
薇奥拉　　你猜想得不错,我不是我自己。

OLIVIA	I would you were as I would have you be!
VIOLA	Would it be better, madam, than I am?
	I wish it might, for now I am your fool.
OLIVIA	O, what a deal of scorn looks beautiful
	In the contempt and anger of his lip!
	A murderous guilt shows not itself more soon
	Than love that would seem hid: love's night is noon.
	Cesario, by the roses of the spring,
	By maidhood, honour, truth and every thing,
	I love thee so, that, maugre all thy pride,
	Nor wit nor reason can my passion hide.
	Do not extort thy reasons from this clause,
	For that I woo, thou therefore hast no cause,
	But rather reason thus with reason fetter,
	Love sought is good, but given unsought better.
VIOLA	By innocence I swear, and by my youth
	I have one heart, one bosom and one truth,
	And that no woman has; nor never none
	Shall mistress be of it, save I alone.
	And so adieu, good madam: never more
	Will I my master's tears to you deplore.
OLIVIA	Yet come again; for thou perhaps mayst move that heart,
	which now abhors, to like his love.

Exeunt.

奥丽维娅　　我希望你是我所希望于你的那种人!

薇奥拉　　　那是不是比现在的我要好些,小姐?我希望好一些,因为现在我不过是你的弄人。

奥丽维娅　　唉!他嘴角的轻蔑和怒气,
　　　　　　冷然的神态可多么美丽!
　　　　　　爱比杀人重罪更难隐藏;
　　　　　　爱的黑夜有中午的阳光。
　　　　　　西萨里奥,凭着春日蔷薇、
　　　　　　贞操、忠信与一切,我爱你
　　　　　　这样真诚,不顾你的骄傲,
　　　　　　理智拦不住热情的宣告。
　　　　　　别以为我这样向你求情,
　　　　　　你就可以无须再献殷勤;
　　　　　　须知求得的爱虽费心力,
　　　　　　不劳而获的更应该珍惜。

薇奥拉　　　我起誓,凭着天真与青春,
　　　　　　我只有一条心一片忠诚,
　　　　　　没有女人能够把它占有,
　　　　　　只有我是我自己的君后。
　　　　　　别了,小姐,我从此不再
　　　　　　来为我主人向你苦苦陈哀。

奥丽维娅　　你不妨再来,也许能感动
　　　　　　我释去憎嫌把感情珍重。

　　　　　　　　　　　同下。

SCENE II

A room in OLIVIA's house.
Enter SIR TOBY BELCH, SIR ANDREW AGUECHEEK and FABIAN.

SIR ANDREW No, faith, I'll not stay a jot longer.

SIR TOBY Thy reason, dear venom, give thy reason.

FABIAN You must needs yield your reason, Sir Andrew.

SIR ANDREW Marry, I saw your niece do more favours to the count's serving-man than ever she bestowed upon me;
I saw't i' the orchard.

SIR TOBY Did she see thee the while, old boy? tell me that.

SIR ANDREW As plain as I see you now.

FABIAN This was a great argument of love in her toward you.

SIR ANDREW 'Slight, will you make an ass o' me?

FABIAN I will prove it legitimate, sir, upon the oaths of judgment and reason.

SIR TOBY And they have been grand-jury-men since before Noah was a sailor.

FABIAN She did show favour to the youth in your sight only to exasperate you, to awake your dormouse valour, to put fire in your heart and brimstone in your liver. You should then have accosted her; and with some excellent jests, fire-new from the mint, you should have banged the youth into dumbness. This was looked for at your hand, and this was balked: the double gilt of this opportunity you let time wash off, and you are now sailed into the north of my lady's opinion; where you will hang like an icicle on a Dutchman's beard, unless you do redeem it by some laudable attempt either of valour or policy.

SIR ANDREW An't be any way, it must be with valour; for policy I hate: I

第二场

奥丽维娅宅中一室。

托比·培尔契爵士，安德鲁·艾古契克爵士及费边上。

安德鲁　　不，真的，我再不能住下去了。

托　比　　为什么呢，恼火的朋友？说出你的理由来。

费　边　　是啊，安德鲁爵士，您得说出个理由来。

安德鲁　　嘿，我见你的侄小姐对待那个公爵的佣人比之待我好得多。我在花园里瞧见的。

托　比　　她那时也看见你吗，老兄？告诉我。

安德鲁　　就像我现在看见你一样明白。

费　边　　那正是她爱您的一个很好的证据。

安德鲁　　啐！你把我当作一头驴子吗？

费　边　　大人，我可以用判断和推理来证明这句话的不错。

托　比　　说得好，判断和推理在挪亚①还没有上船以前，已经就当上陪审官了。

费　边　　她当着您的面对那个少年表示殷勤，是要叫您发急，唤醒您那打瞌睡的勇气，给您的心里燃起火来，在您的肝脏里加点儿硫磺罢了。您那时就该走上去向她招呼，说几句崭新的俏皮话儿叫那年轻人哑口无言。她盼望您这样，可是您却大意错过了。您放过了这么一个大好的机会，我的小姐自然要冷淡您啦；您目前在她心里的地位就像挂在荷兰人胡须上的冰柱一样，除非您能用勇气或是手段干出一些出色的勾当，才可以挽回过来。

安德鲁　　无论如何，我宁愿用勇气。因为我顶讨厌使手段。叫我做个政客，还不如做个布朗派②的教徒。

---

① 挪亚（Noah）及其方舟的故事，见《圣经》，《创世纪》第六章。
② 布朗派为英国伊丽莎白时代清教徒布朗（Robert Browne）所创的教派。

	had as lief be a Brownist as a politician.
SIR TOBY	Why, then, build me thy fortunes upon the basis of valour. Challenge me the count's youth to fight with him; hurt him in eleven places: my niece shall take note of it; and assure thyself, there is no love-broker in the world can more prevail in man's commendation with woman than report of valour.
FABIAN	There is no way but this, Sir Andrew.
SIR ANDREW	Will either of you bear me a challenge to him?
SIR TOBY	Go, write it in a martial hand; be curst and brief; it is no matter how witty, so it be eloquent and fun of invention: taunt him with the licence of ink: if thou thou'st him some thrice, it shall not be amiss; and as many lies as will lie in thy sheet of paper, although the sheet were big enough for the bed of Ware in England, set 'em down: go, about it. Let there be gall enough in thy ink, though thou write with a goose-pen, no matter: about it.
SIR ANDREW	Where shall I find you?
SIR TOBY	We'll call thee at the cubiculo: go.

Exit SIR ANDREW.

FABIAN	This is a dear manikin to you, Sir Toby.
SIR TOBY	I have been dear to him, lad, some two thousand strong, or so.
FABIAN	We shall have a rare letter from him: but you'll not deliver't?
SIR TOBY	Never trust me, then; and by all means stir on the youth to an answer. I think oxen and wainropes cannot hale them together. For Andrew, if he were opened, and you find so much blood in his liver as will clog the foot of a flea, I'll eat the rest of the anatomy.
FABIAN	And his opposite, the youth, bears in his visage no great presage of cruelty.

托　比	好啊,那么把你的命运建筑在勇气上吧。给我去向那公爵差来的少年挑战,在他身上戳十来个窟窿,我的侄女一定会注意到。你可以相信,世上没有一个媒人会比一个勇敢的名声更能说动女人的心了。
费　边	此外可没有别的办法了,安德鲁大人。
安德鲁	你们谁肯替我向他下战书?
托　比	快去用一手虎虎有威的笔法写起来。要干脆简单,不用说俏皮话,只要言之成理,别出心裁就得了。尽你的笔墨所能把他嘲骂;要是你把他"你"啊"你"的"你"了三四次,那不会有错;再把纸上写满了谎言,即使你的纸大得足以铺满英国威尔地方的那张大床①。快去写吧。把你的墨水里掺满着怨毒,虽然你用的是一枝鹅毛笔。去吧。
安德鲁	我到什么地方来见你们?
托　比	我们会到你房间里来看你;去吧。

安德鲁下。

费　边	这是您的一个宝货,托比老爷。
托　比	我倒累他破费过不少呢,孩儿,约莫有两千多块钱的样子。
费　边	我们就可以看到他的一封妙信了。可是您不会给他送去的吧?
托　比	要是我不送去,你别相信我;我一定要把那年轻人激出一个回音来。我想就是叫牛儿拉着车绳也拉不拢他们两人在一起。你把安德鲁解剖开来,要是能在他肝脏里找得出一滴可以沾湿一只跳蚤的脚的血,我愿意把他那副臭皮囊吃下去。
费　边	他那个对头的年轻人,照那副相貌看来,也不像是会下辣手的。

---

① 该床方十一呎,今尚存。

Enter MARIA.

SIR TOBY Look, where the youngest wren of nine comes.

MARIA If you desire the spleen, and will laugh yourself into stitches, follow me. Yond gull Malvolio is turned heathen, a very renegado; for there is no Christian, that means to be saved by believing rightly, can ever believe such impossible passages of grossness. He's in yellow stockings.

SIR TOBY And cross-gartered?

MARIA Most villanously; like a pedant that keeps a school i' the church. I have dogged him, like his murderer. He does obey every point of the letter that I dropped to betray him: he does smile his face into more lines than is in the new map with the augmentation of the Indies: you have not seen such a thing as 'tis. I can hardly forbear hurling things at him. I know my lady will strike him: if she do, he'll smile and take't for a great favour.

SIR TOBY Come, bring us, bring us where he is.

Exeunt.

玛利娅上。

托 比　　瞧，一窠九只的鹡鸰中顶小的一只来了。

玛利娅　　要是你们愿意捧腹大笑，不怕笑到腰酸背痛，那么跟我来吧。那只蠢鹅马伏里奥已经信了邪道，变成一个十足的异教徒了；因为没有一个相信正道而希望得救的基督徒，会做出这种丑恶不堪的奇形怪状来的。他穿着黄袜子呢。

托 比　　袜带是十字交叉的吗？

玛利娅　　再难看不过的了，就像个在寺院里开学堂的塾师先生。我像是他的刺客一样紧跟着他。我故意掉下来诱他的那封信上的话，他每一句都听从；他笑容满面，脸上的皱纹比增添了东印度群岛的新地图上的线纹还多。你们从来不曾见过这样一个东西；我真忍不住要向他丢东西过去。我知道小姐一定会打他；要是她打了他，他一定仍然会笑，以为是一件大恩典。

托 比　　来，带我们去，带我们到他那儿去。

同下。

SCENE III

A street.
Enter SEBASTIAN and ANTONIO.

SEBASTIAN I would not by my will have troubled you;
But, since you make your pleasure of your pains,
I will no further chide you.

ANTONIO I could not stay behind you: my desire,
More sharp than filed steel, did spur me forth;
And not all love to see you, though so much
As might have drawn one to a longer voyage,
But jealousy what might befall your travel,
Being skilless in these parts; which to a stranger,
Unguided and unfriended, often prove
Rough and unhospitable: my willing love,
The rather by these arguments of fear,
Set forth in your pursuit.

SEBASTIAN My kind Antonio,
I can no other answer make but thanks,
And thanks; and ever thanks;and oft good turns
Are shuffled off with such uncurrent pay:
But, were my worth as is my conscience firm,
You should find better dealing. What's to do?
Shall we go see the reliques of this town?

ANTONIO To-morrow, sir: best first go see your lodging.

SEBASTIAN I am not weary, and 'tis long to night:
I pray you, let us satisfy our eyes
With the memorials and the things of fame
That do renown this city.

ANTONIO Would you'ld pardon me;
I do not without danger walk these streets:

第三场

街道。
西巴斯辛及安东尼奥上。

西巴斯辛 我本来不愿意麻烦你,可是你既然这样欢喜自己劳碌,那么我也不再向你多话了。

安东尼奥 我抛不下你,我的愿望比磨过的刀还要锐利地驱迫着我。虽然为了要看见你,再远的路我也会跟着你去,可并不全然为着这个理由:我担心你在这些地方是个陌生人,路上也许会碰到些什么;一路没人领导没有朋友的异乡客,出门总有许多不方便。我的诚心的爱,再加上这样使我忧虑的理由,迫使我来追赶你。

西巴斯辛 我的善良的安东尼奥,除了感谢、感谢、永远的感谢之外,再没有别的话好回答你了。一件好事常常只换得一声空口的道谢;可是我的钱财假如能跟我的衷心的感谢一样多,你的好心一定不会得不到重重的酬报。我们干些什么呢?要不要去瞧瞧这城里的古迹?

安东尼奥 明天吧,先生,还是先去找个下处。
西巴斯辛 我并不疲倦,到天黑还有许多时候呢,让我们去瞧瞧这儿的名胜,一饱眼福吧。

安东尼奥 请你原谅我,我在这一带街道上走路是冒着危险的。从前我曾经参加海战,和公爵的舰队作过对,那时我很立了一点功,假如在

	Once, in a sea-fight, 'gainst the count his galleys
	I did some service; of such note indeed,
	That were I ta'en here it would scarce be answer'd.
SEBASTIAN	Belike you slew great number of his people.
ANTONIO	The offence is not of such a bloody nature;
	Albeit the quality of the time and quarrel
	Might well have given us bloody argument.
	It might have since been answer'd in repaying
	What we took from them; which, for traffic's sake,
	Most of our city did: only myself stood out;
	For which, if I be lapsed in this place,
	I shall pay dear.
SEBASTIAN	Do not then walk too open.
ANTONIO	It doth not fit me. Hold, sir, here's my purse.
	In the south suburbs, at the Elephant,
	Is best to lodge: I will bespeak our diet,
	Whiles you beguile the time and feed your knowledge
	With viewing of the town: there shall you have me.
SEBASTIAN	Why I your purse?
ANTONIO	Haply your eye shall light upon some toy
	You have desire to purchase; and your store,
	I think, is not for idle markets, sir.
SEBASTIAN	I'll be your purse-bearer and leave you
	For an hour.
ANTONIO	To the Elephant.
SEBASTIAN	I do remember.

Exeunt.

这儿给捉到了,可不知要怎样抵罪哩。

西巴斯辛　　大概你杀死了很多的人吧?
安东尼奥　　我的罪名并不是这么一种杀人流血的性质;虽然照那时的情形和争执的激烈看来,很容易有流血的可能。本来把我们夺来的东西还给了他们,就可以和平解决了,我们城里大多数人为了经商,也都这样做了;可是我却不肯屈服,因此,要是我在这儿给捉到了的话,他们决不会轻轻放过我。

西巴斯辛　　那么你不要太出来招摇吧。
安东尼奥　　那的确不大妥当。先生,这儿是我的钱袋,请你拿着吧。南郊的大象旅店是最好的下宿的地方,我先去定好膳宿;你可以在城里逛着见识见识,再到那边来见我好了。

西巴斯辛　　为什么你要把你的钱袋给我?
安东尼奥　　也许你会看中什么玩意儿想要买下;我知道你的钱不够买这些非急用的东西,先生。

西巴斯辛　　好,我就替你保管你的钱袋,过一个钟头再见吧。

安东尼奥　　在大象旅店。
西巴斯辛　　我记得。

各下。

SCENE IV

OLIVIA's garden.
Enter OLIVIA and MARIA.

OLIVIA I have sent after him: he says he'll come;
How shall I feast him? what bestow of him?
For youth is bought more oft than begg'd or borrow'd.
I speak too loud.
Where is Malvolio? he is sad and civil,
And suits well for a servant with my fortunes:
Where is Malvolio?

MARIA He's coming, madam; but in very strange manner. He is, sure, possessed, madam.

OLIVIA Why, what's the matter? does he rave?

MARIA No. madam, he does nothing but smile: your ladyship were best to have some guard about you, if he come; for, sure, the man is tainted in's wits.

OLIVIA Go call him hither.

Exit MARIA.

I am as mad as he,
If sad and merry madness equal be.

Re-enter MARIA, with MALVOLIO.

How now, Malvolio!

MALVOLIO Sweet lady, ho, ho.

OLIVIA Smil'st thou?
I sent for thee upon a sad occasion.

MALVOLIO Sad, lady! I could be sad: this does make some obstruction in the blood, this cross-gartering; but what of that? if it please the eye of one, it is with me as the very true sonnet

第四场

奥丽维娅的花园。

奥丽维娅及玛利娅上。

奥丽维娅　　我已经差人去请他了。假如他肯来,我要怎样款待他呢?我要给他些什么呢?因为年轻人常常是买来的,而不是讨来或借来的。我说得太高声了。马伏里奥在哪儿呢?他这人很严肃,懂得规矩,以我目前的处境来说,很配做我的仆人。马伏里奥在什么地方?

玛　利　娅　　他就来了,小姐;可是他的样子古怪得很。他一定给鬼迷了,小姐。

奥丽维娅　　啊,怎么啦?他在说胡话吗?

玛　利　娅　　不,小姐;他只是一味笑。他来的时候,小姐,您最好叫人保护着您,因为这人的神经有点不正常呢。

奥丽维娅　　去叫他来。

玛利娅下。

他是痴汉,我也是个疯婆;
他欢喜,我忧愁,一样糊涂。

玛利娅偕马伏里奥重上。

怎样,马伏里奥!

马伏里奥　　亲爱的小姐,哈哈!

奥丽维娅　　你笑吗?我要差你做一件正经事呢,别那么快活。

马伏里奥　　不快活,小姐!我当然可以不快活,这种十字交叉的袜带扎得我血脉不通,可是那有什么要紧?只要能叫一个人看了欢喜,那就像诗上所说的"一人欢喜,人人欢喜"了。

	is, 'Please one, and please all.'
OLIVIA	Why, how dost thou, man? what is the matter with thee?
MALVOLIO	Not black in my mind, though yellow in my legs. It did come to his hands, and commands shall be executed: I think we do know the sweet Roman hand.
OLIVIA	Wilt thou go to bed, Malvolio?
MALVOLIO	To bed! ay, sweet-heart, and I'll come to thee.
OLIVIA	God comfort thee! Why dost thou smile so and kiss thy hand so oft?
MARIA	How do you, Malvolio?
MALVOLIO	At your request! yes; nightingales answer daws.
MARIA	Why appear you with this ridiculous boldness before my lady?
MALVOLIO	'Be not afraid of greatness:' 'twas well writ.
OLIVIA	What meanest thou by that, Malvolio?
MALVOLIO	'Some are born great,'—
OLIVIA	Ha!
MALVOLIO	'Some achieve greatness,'—
OLIVIA	What sayest thou?
MALVOLIO	'And some have greatness thrust upon them.'
OLIVIA	Heaven restore thee!
MALVOLIO	'Remember who commended thy yellow stockings,'—
OLIVIA	Thy yellow stockings!
MALVOLIO	'And wished to see thee cross-gartered.'
OLIVIA	Cross-gartered!
MALVOLIO	'Go to thou art made, if thou desirest to be so;'—
OLIVIA	Am I made?
MALVOLIO	'If not, let me see thee a servant still.'
OLIVIA	Why, this is very midsummer madness.

Enter Servant.

Servant	Madam, the young gentleman of the Count Orsino's is

奥丽维娅	什么，你怎么啦，家伙？究竟是怎么一回事？
马伏里奥	我的腿儿虽然是黄的，我的心儿却不黑。那信已经到了他的手里，命令一定要服从。我想那一手簪花妙楷我们都是认得出来的。
奥丽维娅	你还是睡觉去吧，马伏里奥。
马伏里奥	睡觉去！对了，好人儿，我一定奉陪。
奥丽维娅	上帝保佑你！为什么你这样笑着，还老是吻你的手？
玛利娅	您怎么啦，马伏里奥？
马伏里奥	多承见问！是的，夜莺应该回答乌鸦的问话。
玛利娅	您为什么当着小姐的面前这样放肆？
马伏里奥	"不用惧怕富贵，"写得很好！
奥丽维娅	你说那话是什么意思，马伏里奥？
马伏里奥	"有的人是生来的富贵，"——
奥丽维娅	嘿！
马伏里奥	"有的人是挣来的富贵，"——
奥丽维娅	你说什么？
马伏里奥	"有的人是送上来的富贵。"
奥丽维娅	上天保佑你！
马伏里奥	"记着谁曾经赞美过你的黄袜子，"——
奥丽维娅	你的黄袜子！
马伏里奥	"愿意看见你永远扎着十字交叉的袜带。"
奥丽维娅	扎着十字交叉的袜带！
马伏里奥	"好，只要你自己愿意，你就可以出头了，"——
奥丽维娅	我就可以出头了？
马伏里奥	"否则让我见你一生一世做个管家吧。"
奥丽维娅	哎哟，这家伙简直中了暑在发疯了。

一仆人上。

仆人	小姐，奥西诺公爵的那位青年使者回来了，我好容易才请他回

	returned: I could hardly entreat him back: he attends your ladyship's pleasure.
OLIVIA	I'll come to him.

Exit Servant.

Good Maria, let this fellow be looked to. Where's my cousin Toby? Let some of my people have a special care of him: I would not have him miscarry for the half of my dowry.

Exeunt OLIVIA and MARIA.

MALVOLIO	Oh, ho! do you come near me now? no worse man than Sir Toby to look to me! This concurs directly with the letter: she sends him on purpose, that I may appear stubborn to him; for she incites me to that in the letter. 'Cast thy humble slough,' says she; 'be opposite with a kinsman, surly with servants; let thy tongue tang with arguments of state; put thyself into the trick of singularity;' and consequently sets down the manner how; as, a sad face, a reverend carriage, a slow tongue, in the habit of some sir of note, and so forth. I have limed her; but it is Jove's doing, and Jove make me thankful! And when she went away now, 'Let this fellow be looked to:' fellow! not Malvolio, nor after my degree, but fellow. Why, every thing adheres together, that no dram of a scruple, no scruple of a scruple, no obstacle, no incredulous or unsafe circumstance— What can be said? Nothing that can be can come between me and the full prospect of my hopes. Well, Jove, not I, is the doer of this, and he is to be thanked.

Re-enter MARIA, with SIR TOBY BELCH and FABIAN.

SIR TOBY	Which way is he, in the name of sanctity? If all the devils of

来。他在等候着小姐的意旨。

奥丽维娅　我就去见他。

仆人下。

好玛利娅，这家伙要好好看管。我的托比叔父呢？叫几个人加意留心着他；我宁可失掉我嫁妆的一半，也不希望看到他有什么意外。

奥丽维娅、玛利娅下。

马伏里奥　啊，哈哈！你现在明白了吗？不叫别人，却叫托比爵士来照看我！我正合信上所说的：她有意叫他来，好让我跟他顶撞一下，因为她信里正要我这样。"脱去你卑恭的旧习；"她说，"对亲戚不妨分庭抗礼，对仆人不妨摆摆架子；你嘴里要鼓唇弄舌地谈些国家大事，装出一副矜持的样子；"随后还写着怎样装出一副严肃的面孔、庄重的举止、慢声慢气的说话腔调，学着大人先生的样子，诸如此类。我已经捉到她了，可是那是上帝的功劳，感谢上帝！而且她刚才临去的时候，她说，"这家伙要好好看管；"家伙！不说马伏里奥，也不照我的地位称呼我，而叫我家伙。哈哈，一切都符合，一点儿没有疑惑，一点儿没有阻碍，一点儿没有不放心的地方。还有什么好说呢？什么也不能阻止我达到我的全部的希望。好，干这种事情的是上帝，不是我，感谢上帝！

玛利娅偕托比·培尔契爵士及费边上。

托　　比　凭着神圣的名义，他在哪儿？要是地狱里的群鬼都缩小了身子，

	hell be drawn in little, and Legion himself possessed him, yet I'll speak to him.
FABIAN	Here he is, here he is. How is't with you, sir? how is't with you, man?
MALVOLIO	Go off; I discard you: let me enjoy my private: go off.
MARIA	Lo, how hollow the fiend speaks within him! did not I tell you? Sir Toby, my lady prays you to have a care of him.
MALVOLIO	Ah, ha! does she so?
SIR TOBY	Go to, go to; peace, peace; we must deal gently with him: let me alone. How do you, Malvolio? how is't with you? What, man! defy the devil: consider, he's an enemy to mankind.
MALVOLIO	Do you know what you say?
MARIA	La you, an you speak ill of the devil, how he takes it at heart! Pray God, he be not bewitched!
FABIAN	Carry his water to the wise woman.
MARIA	Marry, and it shall be done to-morrow morning, if I live. My lady would not lose him for more than I'll say.
MALVOLIO	How now, mistress!
MARIA	O Lord!
SIR TOBY	Prithee, hold thy peace; this is not the way: do you not see you move him? let me alone with him.
FABIAN	No way but gentleness; gently, gently: the fiend is rough, and will not be roughly used.
SIR TOBY	Why, how now, my bawcock! how dost thou, chuck?
MALVOLIO	Sir!
SIR TOBY	Ay, Biddy, come with me. What, man! 'tis not for gravity to play at cherry-pit with Satan: hang him, foul collier!
MARIA	Get him to say his prayers, good Sir Toby, get him to pray.
MALVOLIO	My prayers, minx!
MARIA	No, I warrant you, he will not hear of godliness.
MALVOLIO	Go, hang yourselves all! you are idle shallow things: I am

　　　　　　　一起走进他的身体里去，我也要跟他说话。

费　　边　　他在这儿，他在这儿。您怎么啦，大爷？您怎么啦，老兄？

马伏里奥　　走开，我用不着你。别搅扰了我的安静。走开！
玛 利 娅　　听，魔鬼在他嘴里说着鬼话了！我不是对您说过吗？托比老爷，小姐请您看顾看顾他。
马伏里奥　　啊！啊！她这样说吗？
托　　比　　好了，好了，别闹了吧！我们一定要客客气气对付他；让我一个人来吧。——你好，马伏里奥？你怎么啦？嘿，老兄！抵抗魔鬼呀！你想，他是人类的仇敌呢。
马伏里奥　　你知道你在说些什么话吗？
玛 利 娅　　你们瞧！你们一说了魔鬼的坏话，他就生气了。求求上帝，不要让他中了鬼迷才好！
费　　边　　把他的小便送到巫婆那边去吧。
玛 利 娅　　好，明天早晨一定送去。我的小姐舍不得他哩。

马伏里奥　　怎么，姑娘！
玛 利 娅　　主啊！
托　　比　　请你别闹，这不是个办法；你不见你惹他生气了吗？让我来对付他。
费　　边　　除了用软功之外，没有别的法子。轻轻地、轻轻地，魔鬼是个粗坯，你要跟他动粗是不行的。
托　　比　　喂，怎么啦，我的好家伙！你好，好人儿？
马伏里奥　　爵士！
托　　比　　哦，小鸡，跟我来吧。嘿，老兄！跟魔鬼在一起玩可不对。该死的黑鬼！
玛 利 娅　　叫他念祈祷，好托比老爷，叫他祈祷。
马伏里奥　　念祈祷，小淫妇！
玛 利 娅　　你们听着，跟他讲到关于上帝的话，他就听不进去了。
马伏里奥　　你们全给我去上吊吧！你们都是些浅薄无聊的东西；我不是跟你

not of your element: you shall know more hereafter.

Exit.

SIR TOBY   Is't possible?

FABIAN   If this were played upon a stage now, I could condemn it as an improbable fiction.

SIR TOBY   His very genius hath taken the infection of the device, man.

MARIA   Nay, pursue him now, lest the device take air and taint.

FABIAN   Why, we shall make him mad indeed.

MARIA   The house will be the quieter.

SIR TOBY   Come, we'll have him in a dark room and bound. My niece is already in the belief that he's mad: we may carry it thus, for our pleasure and his penance, till our very pastime, tired out of breath, prompt us to have mercy on him: at which time we will bring the device to the bar and crown thee for a finder of madmen. But see, but see.

Enter SIR ANDREW.

FABIAN   More matter for a May morning.

SIR ANDREW   Here's the challenge, read it: warrant there's vinegar and pepper in't.

FABIAN   Is't so saucy?

SIR ANDREW   Ay, is't, I warrant him: do but read.

SIR TOBY   Give me.

    [Reads] 'Youth, whatsoever thou art, thou art but a scurvy fellow.'

FABIAN   Good, and valiant.

SIR TOBY   *[Reads]* 'Wonder not, nor admire not in thy mind, why I do call thee so, for I will show thee no reason for't.'

FABIAN   A good note; that keeps you from the blow of the law.

SIR TOBY   *[Reads]* 'Thou comest to the lady Olivia, and in my sight

们一样的人。你们就会知道的。

下。

托　　比	有这等事吗？
费　　边	要是这种情形在舞台上表演起来，我一定要批评它捏造得出乎情理之外。
托　　比	这个计策已经把他迷得神魂颠倒了，老兄。
玛利娅	还是追上他去吧，也许这计策一漏了风，就会毁掉。
费　　边	哦，我们真的要叫他发起疯来。
玛利娅	那时屋子里可以清静些。
托　　比	来，我们要把他捆起来关在一间暗室里。我的侄女已经相信他疯了；我们可以这样依计而行，让我们开开心，叫他吃吃苦头。等到我们开腻了这玩笑，再向他发起慈悲来，那时我们宣布我们的计策，把你封作疯人的发现者。可是瞧，瞧！

安德鲁·艾古契克爵士上。

费　　边	又有别的花样来了。
安德鲁	挑战书已经写好在此，你读读看。念上去就像酸醋胡椒的味道呢。
费　　边	是这样厉害吗？
安德鲁	对了，我向他保证的。你只要读着好了。
托　　比	给我。 （读）"年轻人，不管你是谁，你不过是个下贱的东西。"
费　　边	好，真勇敢！
托　　比	"不要吃惊，也不要奇怪为什么我这样称呼你，因为我不愿告诉你是什么理由。"
费　　边	一句很好的话，这样您就可以不受法律的攻击了。
托　　比	"你来见奥丽维娅小姐，她当着我的面把你厚待。可是你说谎，

	she uses thee kindly: but thou liest in thy throat; that is not the matter I challenge thee for.'
FABIAN	Very brief, and to exceeding good sense—less.
SIR TOBY	*[Reads]* 'I will waylay thee going home; where if it be thy chance to kill me,'—
FABIAN	Good.
SIR TOBY	*[Reads]* 'Thou killest me like a rogue and a villain.'
FABIAN	Still you keep o' the windy side of the law: good.
SIR TOBY	*[Reads]* 'Fare thee well; and God have mercy upon one of our souls! He may have mercy upon mine; but my hope is better, and so look to thyself. Thy friend, as thou usest him, and thy sworn enemy, ANDREW AGUECHEEK.' If this letter move him not, his legs cannot: I'll give't him.
MARIA	You may have very fit occasion for't: he is now in some commerce with my lady, and will by and by depart.
SIR TOBY	Go, Sir Andrew: scout me for him at the corner of the orchard like a bum-baily: so soon as ever thou seest him, draw; and, as thou drawest swear horrible; for it comes to pass oft that a terrible oath, with a swaggering accent sharply twanged off, gives manhood more approbation than ever proof itself would have earned him. Away!
SIR ANDREW	Nay, let me alone for swearing.

Exit.

SIR TOBY	Now will not I deliver his letter: for the behavior of the young gentleman gives him out to be of good capacity and breeding; his employment between his lord and my niece confirms no less: therefore this letter, being so excellently ignorant, will breed no terror in the youth: he will find it comes from a clodpole. But, sir, I will deliver his challenge

那并不是我要向你挑战的理由。"

费　边		很简单明白，而且百分之百地——不通。
托　比		（读）"我要在你回去的时候埋伏着等候你。要是命该你把我杀死的话——"
费　边		很好。
托　比		"你便是个坏蛋和恶人。"
费　边		您仍旧避过了法律方面的责任，很好。
托　比		（读）"再会吧；上帝超度我们两人中一人的灵魂吧！也许他会超度我的灵魂；可是我比你有希望一些，所以你留心着自己吧。你的朋友（这要看你怎样对待他），和你的势不两立的仇敌，安德鲁·艾古契克。" ——要是这封信不能激动他，那么他的两条腿也不能走动了。我去送给他。
玛利娅		您有很凑巧的机会，他现在正在跟小姐谈话，等会儿就要出来了。
托　比		去，安德鲁大人，给我在园子角落里等着他，像个衙役似的；一看见他，便拔出剑来；一拔剑，就高声咒骂；一句可怕的咒骂，神气活现地从嘴里厉声发出来，比之真才实艺更能叫人相信他是个了不得的家伙。去吧！
安德鲁		好，骂人的事情我自己会。

下。

托　比		我可不去送这封信。因为照这位青年的举止看来，是个很有资格很有教养的人，否则他的主人不会差他来拉拢我的侄女的。这封信写得那么奇妙不通，一定不会叫这青年害怕；他一定会以为这是一个呆子写的。可是，老兄，我要口头去替他挑战，故意夸张艾古契克的勇气，让这位仁兄相信他是个勇猛暴躁的家伙。我知道他那样年轻一定会害怕起来的。这样他们两人便会彼此害怕，

by word of mouth; set upon Aguecheek a notable report of valour; and drive the gentleman, as I know his youth will aptly receive it, into a most hideous opinion of his rage, skill, fury and impetuosity. This will so fright them both that they will kill one another by the look, like cockatrices.

Re-enter OLIVIA, with VIOLA.

FABIAN Here he comes with your niece: give them way till he take leave, and presently after him.

SIR TOBY I will meditate the while upon some horrid message for a challenge.

Exeunt SIR TOBY BELCH, FABIAN, and MARIA.

OLIVIA I have said too much unto a heart of stone
And laid mine honour too unchary out:
There's something in me that reproves my fault;
But such a headstrong potent fault it is,
That it but mocks reproof.

VIOLA With the same havior that your passion bears
Goes on my master's grief.

OLIVIA Here, wear this jewel for me, 'tis my picture;
Refuse it not; it hath no tongue to vex you;
And I beseech you come again to-morrow.
What shall you ask of me that I'll deny,
That honour saved may upon asking give?

VIOLA Nothing but this; your true love for my master.

OLIVIA How with mine honour may I give him that
Which I have given to you?

VIOLA I will acquit you.

OLIVIA Well, come again to-morrow: fare thee well:
A fiend like thee might bear my soul to hell.

就像眼光能杀人的毒蜥蜴似的，两人一照面，就都呜呼哀哉了。

奥丽维娅偕薇奥拉重上。

费　　边　他和您的侄小姐来了。让我们回避他们，等他告别之后再追上去。

托　　比　我可以想出几句可怕的挑战话儿来。

托比、费边、玛丽娅下。

奥丽维娅　我对一颗石子样的心太多费唇舌了，鲁莽地把我的名誉下了赌注。我心里有些埋怨自己的错，可是那是个极其倔强的错，埋怨只能招它一阵讪笑。

薇 奥 拉　我主人的悲哀也正和您这种痴情的样子相同。

奥丽维娅　拿着，为我的缘故把这玩意儿戴在你身上吧，那上面有我的小像。不要拒绝它，它不会多话讨你厌的。请你明天再过来。你无论向我要什么，只要于我的名誉没有妨碍，我都可以给你。

薇 奥 拉　我向您要的，只是请您把真心的爱给我的主人。
奥丽维娅　那我已经给了你了，怎么还能凭着我的名誉再给他呢？

薇 奥 拉　我可以奉还给你。
奥丽维娅　好，明天再来吧。
　　　　　再见！像你这样一个恶魔，我甘愿被你向地狱里拖。

Exit.
Re-enter SIR TOBY BELCH and FABIAN.

SIR TOBY   Gentleman, God save thee.

VIOLA   And you, sir.

SIR TOBY   That defence thou hast, betake thee to't: of what nature the wrongs are thou hast done him, I know not; but thy intercepter, full of despite, bloody as the hunter, attends thee at the orchard-end: dismount thy tuck, be yare in thy preparation, for thy assailant is quick, skilful and deadly.

VIOLA   You mistake, sir; I am sure no man hath any quarrel to me: my remembrance is very free and clear from any image of offence done to any man.

SIR TOBY   You'll find it otherwise, I assure you: therefore, if you hold your life at any price, betake you to your guard; for your opposite hath in him what youth, strength, skill and wrath can furnish man withal.

VIOLA   I pray you, sir, what is he?

SIR TOBY   He is knight, dubbed with unhatched rapier and on carpet consideration; but he is a devil in private brawl: souls and bodies hath he divorced three; and his incensement at this moment is so implacable, that satisfaction can be none but by pangs of death and sepulchre. Hob, nob, is his word; give't or take't.

VIOLA   I will return again into the house and desire some conduct of the lady. I am no fighter. I have heard of some kind of men that put quarrels purposely on others, to taste their valour: belike this is a man of that quirk.

SIR TOBY   Sir, no; his indignation derives itself out of a very competent injury: therefore, get you on and give him his desire. Back you shall not to the house, unless you undertake that with

下。
托比·培尔契爵士及费边重上。

托　　比　　先生,上帝保佑你!

薇奥拉　　上帝保佑您,爵士!

托　　比　　准备着防御吧。我不知道你做了什么对不起他的事情,可是你那位对头满心怀恨,一股子的杀气在园子尽头等着你呢。拔出你的剑来,赶快预备好,因为你的敌人是个敏捷精明而可怕的人。

薇奥拉　　您弄错了,爵士,我相信没人会跟我争吵;我完全不记得我曾经得罪过什么人。

托　　比　　你会知道事情是恰恰相反的,我告诉你。所以要是你看重你的生命的话,留点神吧;因为你的冤家年轻力壮,武艺不凡,火气又那么大。

薇奥拉　　请问爵士,他是谁呀?

托　　比　　他是个不靠军功而受封的骑士,可是跟人吵起架来,那简直是个魔鬼:他已经叫三个人的灵魂出壳了。现在他的怒气已经一发而不可收拾,非把人杀死送进坟墓里去决不甘心。他的格言是不管三七二十一,拼个你死我活。

薇奥拉　　我要回到府里去请小姐派几个人给我保镖。我不会跟人打架。我听说有些人故意向别人寻事,试验他们的勇气,这个人大概也是这一类的。

托　　比　　不,先生,他的发怒是有充分理由的,因为你得罪了他,所以你还是上去答应他的要求吧。你不能回到屋子里去,除非你在没有跟他交手之前先跟我比个高低。横竖都得冒险,你何必不去会会

	me which with as much safety you might answer him: therefore, on, or strip your sword stark naked; for meddle you must, that's certain, or forswear to wear iron about you.
VIOLA	This is as uncivil as strange. I beseech you, do me this courteous office, as to know of the knight what my offence to him is: it is something of my negligence, nothing of my purpose.
SIR TOBY	I will do so. Signior Fabian, stay you by this gentleman till my return.

Exit.

VIOLA	Pray you, sir, do you know of this matter?
FABIAN	I know the knight is incensed against you, even to a mortal arbitrement; but nothing of the circumstance more.
VIOLA	I beseech you, what manner of man is he?
FABIAN	Nothing of that wonderful promise, to read him by his form, as you are like to find him in the proof of his valour. He is, indeed, sir, the most skilful, bloody and fatal opposite that you could possibly have found in any part of Illyria. Will you walk towards him? I will make your peace with him if I can.
VIOLA	I shall be much bound to you for't: I am one that had rather go with sir priest than sir knight: I care not who knows so much of my mettle.

Exeunt.
Re-enter SIR TOBY BELCH, with SIR ANDREW.

SIR TOBY	Why, man, he's a very devil; I have not seen such a firago. I had a pass with him, rapier, scabbard and all, and he gives me the stuck in with such a mortal motion, that it is inevitable; and on the answer, he pays you as surely as your

他呢？所以上去吧，把你的剑赤条条地拔出来，无论如何你非得动手不可，否则以后你再不用带剑了。

薇奥拉　　这真是既无礼又古怪。请您帮我一下忙，去问问那骑士我得罪了他什么。那一定是我偶然的疏忽，决不是有意的。

托　比　　我就去问他。费边先生，你陪着这位先生等我回来。

　　　　　　　　　　　下。

薇奥拉　　先生，请问您知道这是怎么一回事吗？
费　边　　我知道那骑士对您很不乐意，抱着拼命的决心，可是详细的情形却不知道。
薇奥拉　　请您告诉我他是个什么样子的人？
费　边　　照他的外表上看起来，并没有什么惊人的地方，可是您跟他一交手，就知道他的厉害了。他，先生，的确是您在伊利里亚无论哪个地方所碰得到的最有本领、最凶狠、最厉害的敌手。您就过去见他好不好？我愿意替您跟他讲和，要是能够的话。

薇奥拉　　那多谢您了。我是个宁愿亲近教士不愿亲近骑士的人。我这副小胆子，即使让别人知道了，我也不在乎。

　　　　　　　　　　同下。
　　　　　　　　托比及安德鲁重上。

托　比　　嘿，老兄，他才是个魔鬼呢；我从来不曾见过这么一个泼货。我跟他连剑带鞘较量了一回，他给我这么致命的一刺，简直无从招架。至于他还起手来，那简直像是你的脚踏在地上一样万无一失。他们说他曾经在波斯王宫里当过剑师。

	feet hit the ground they step on. They say he has been fencer to the Sophy.
SIR ANDREW	Pox on't, I'll not meddle with him.
SIR TOBY	Ay, but he will not now be pacified: Fabian can scarce hold him yonder.
SIR ANDREW	Plague on't, an I thought he had been valiant and so cunning in fence, I'd have seen him damned ere I'd have challenged him. Let him let the matter slip, and I'll give him my horse, grey Capilet.
SIR TOBY	I'll make the motion: stand here, make a good show on't: this shall end without the perdition of souls.

Aside.

Marry, I'll ride your horse as well as I ride you.

Re-enter FABIAN and VIOLA.
To FABIAN.

I have his horse to take up the quarrel:
I have persuaded him the youth's a devil.

FABIAN	He is as horribly conceited of him; and pants and looks pale, as if a bear were at his heels.
SIR TOBY	*[To VIOLA]* There's no remedy, sir; he will fight with you for's oath sake: marry, he hath better bethought him of his quarrel, and he finds that now scarce to be worth talking of: therefore draw, for the supportance of his vow; he protests he will not hurt you.
VIOLA	*[Aside]* Pray God defend me! A little thing would make me tell them how much I lack of a man.
FABIAN	Give ground, if you see him furious.
SIR TOBY	Come, Sir Andrew, there's no remedy; the gentleman will, for his honour's sake, have one bout with you; he cannot by the

安 德 鲁	糟了！我不高兴跟他动手。
托　　比	好，但是他可不肯甘休呢，费边在那边简直拦不住他。
安 德 鲁	该死！早知道他有这种本领，我再也不去惹他的。假如他肯放过这回，我情愿把我的灰色马儿送给他。
托　　比	我去跟他说去。站在这儿，摆出些威势来；这件事情总可以和平了结的。

旁白。

你的马儿少不得要让我来骑，你可大大地给我捉弄了。

费边及薇奥拉重上。
向费边。

我已经叫他把他的马儿送上议和。我已经叫他相信这孩子是个魔鬼。

费　　边	他也是十分害怕他，吓得心惊肉跳脸色发白，像是一头熊追在背后似的。
托　　比	（向薇奥拉）没有法子，先生，他因为已经发过了誓，非得跟你决斗一下不可。他已经把这回吵闹考虑过，认为起因的确是微不足道的。所以为了他所发的誓起见，拔出你的剑来吧，他声明他不会伤害你的。
薇 奥 拉	（旁白）求上帝保佑我！一点点事情就会给他们知道我是不配当男人的。
费　　边	要是你见他势不可当，就让让他吧。
托　　比	来，安德鲁爵士，没有办法，这位先生为了他的名誉起见，不得不跟你较量一下，按着决斗的规则，他不能规避这一回事。可是

	duello avoid it: but he has promised me, as he is a gentleman and a soldier, he will not hurt you. Come on; to't.
SIR ANDREW	Pray God, he keep his oath!
VIOLA	I do assure you, 'tis against my will.

They draw .Enter ANTONIO.

ANTONIO	Put up your sword. If this young gentleman Have done offence, I take the fault on me: If you offend him, I for him defy you.
SIR TOBY	You, sir! why, what are you?
ANTONIO	One, sir, that for his love dares yet do more Than you have heard him brag to you he will.
SIR TOBY	Nay, if you be an undertaker, I am for you.

They draw .Enter Officers.

FABIAN	O good Sir Toby, hold! here come the officers.
SIR TOBY	I'll be with you anon.
VIOLA	Pray, sir, put your sword up, if you please.
SIR ANDREW	Marry, will I, sir; and, for that I promised you,I'll be as good as my word: he will bear you easily and reins well.
First Officer	This is the man; do thy office.
Second Officer	Antonio, I arrest thee at the suit of Count Orsino.
ANTONIO	You do mistake me, sir.
First Officer	No, sir, no jot; I know your favour well, Though now you have no sea-cap on your head. Take him away: he knows I know him well.
ANTONIO	I must obey.

To VIOLA.

This comes with seeking you:
But there's no remedy; I shall answer it.

|安　德　鲁|求上帝让他不要背誓！|
|薇　奥　拉|相信我，这全然不是出于我的本意。（拔剑）|

拔剑。安东尼奥上。

安东尼奥	放下你的剑。要是这位年轻的先生得罪了你，我替他担个不是；要是你得罪了他，我可不肯对你甘休。（拔剑）
托　　比	你，朋友！咦，你是谁呀？
安东尼奥	先生，我是他的好朋友。为了他的缘故，无论什么事情说得出的便做得到。
托　　比	好吧，你既然这样喜欢管人家的闲事，我就奉陪了。

拔剑。二警吏上。

费　　边	啊，好托比老爷，住手吧！警官们来了。
托　　比	过会儿再跟你算账。
薇　奥　拉	（向安德鲁）先生，请你放下你的剑吧。
安　德　鲁	好，放下就放下，朋友，我可以向你担保，我的话说过就算数。那匹马你骑起来准很舒服，它也很听话。
警　吏　甲	就是这个人。执行你的任务吧。
警　吏　乙	安东尼奥，我奉奥西诺公爵之命来逮捕你。
安东尼奥	你看错人了，朋友。
警　吏　甲	不，先生，一点没有错。我很认识你的脸，虽然你现在头上不戴着水手的帽子。——把他带走，他知道我认识他的。
安东尼奥	我只好服从。

向薇奥拉。

这场祸事都是因为要来寻找你而起，可是没有办法，我必得服罪。现在我不得不向你要回我的钱袋了，你预备怎样呢？叫我难

	What will you do, now my necessity
	Makes me to ask you for my purse? It grieves me
	Much more for what I cannot do for you
	Than what befalls myself. You stand amazed;
	But be of comfort.
Second Officer	Come, sir, away.
ANTONIO	I must entreat of you some of that money.
VIOLA	What money, sir?
	For the fair kindness you have show'd me here,
	And, part, being prompted by your present trouble,
	Out of my lean and low ability
	I'll lend you something: my having is not much;
	I'll make division of my present with you:
	Hold, there's half my coffer.
ANTONIO	Will you deny me now?
	Is't possible that my deserts to you
	Can lack persuasion? Do not tempt my misery,
	Lest that it make me so unsound a man
	As to upbraid you with those kindnesses
	That I have done for you.
VIOLA	I know of none;
	Nor know I you by voice or any feature:
	I hate ingratitude more in a man
	Than lying, vainness, babbling, drunkenness,
	Or any taint of vice whose strong corruption
	Inhabits our frail blood.
ANTONIO	O heavens themselves!
Second Officer	Come, sir, I pray you, go.
ANTONIO	Let me speak a little. This youth that you see here
	I snatch'd one half out of the jaws of death,
	Relieved him with such sanctity of love,

过的倒不是我自己的遭遇，而是不能给你尽一点力。你吃惊吗？请你宽心吧。

警吏乙　来，朋友，去吧。
安东尼奥　那笔钱我必须向你要几个。
薇奥拉　什么钱，先生？为了您在这儿对我的好意相助，又看见您现在的不幸，我愿意尽我的微弱的力量借给您几个钱；我是个穷小子，这儿随身带着的钱，可以跟您平分。拿着吧，这是我一半的家私。

安东尼奥　你现在不认识我了吗？难道我给你的好处不能使你心动吗？别看着我倒霉好欺侮，要是激起我的性子来，我也会不顾一切，向你一一数说你的忘恩负义的。

薇奥拉　我一点不知道，您的声音相貌我也完全不认识。我痛恨人们的忘恩，比之痛恨说谎、虚荣、饶舌、酗酒，或是其他存在于脆弱的人心中的陷入的恶德还要厉害。

安东尼奥　唉，天哪！
警吏乙　好了，对不起，朋友，走吧。
安东尼奥　让我再说句话，你们瞧这个孩子，他是我从死神的掌握中夺了来的，我用神圣的爱心照顾着他；我以为他的样子是个好人，才对他那样恭顺。

	And to his image, which methought did promise
	Most venerable worth, did I devotion.
First Officer	What's that to us? The time goes by: away!
ANTONIO	But O how vile an idol proves this god
	Thou hast, Sebastian, done good feature shame.
	In nature there's no blemish but the mind;
	None can be call'd deform'd but the unkind:
	Virtue is beauty, but the beauteous evil
	Are empty trunks o'erflourish'd by the devil.
First Officer	The man grows mad: away with him! Come, come, sir.
ANTONIO	Lead me on.

Exit with Officers.

VIOLA	Methinks his words do from such passion fly,
	That he believes himself: so do not I.
	Prove true, imagination, O, prove true,
	That I, dear brother, be now ta'en for you!
SIR TOBY	Come hither, knight; come hither, Fabian: we'll whisper o'er
	a couplet or two of most sage saws.
VIOLA	He named Sebastian: I my brother know
	Yet living in my glass; even such and so
	In favour was my brother, and he went
	Still in this fashion, colour, ornament,
	For him I imitate: O, if it prove,
	Tempests are kind and salt waves fresh in love.

Exit.

SIR TOBY	A very dishonest paltry boy, and more a coward than a hare: his dishonesty appears in leaving his friend here in necessity and denying him; and for his cowardship, ask Fabian.

警 吏 甲　　那跟我们有什么相干呢？别耽误了时间，去吧！
安东尼奥　　可是唉！这个天神一样的人，原来却是个邪魔外道！西巴斯辛，
　　　　　　你未免太羞辱了你这副好相貌了。
　　　　　　心上的瑕疵是真的垢污；
　　　　　　无情的人才是残废之徒。
　　　　　　善即是美；但美丽的奸恶，
　　　　　　是魔鬼雕就文采的空椟。
警 吏 甲　　这家伙发疯了；带他去吧！来，来，先生。
安东尼奥　　带我去吧。

　　　　　　　　　　　警吏带安东尼奥下。

薇 奥 拉　　他的话儿句句发自衷肠；
　　　　　　他坚持不疑，我意乱心慌。
　　　　　　但愿想象的事果真不错，
　　　　　　是他把妹妹错认作哥哥！
托　　比　　过来，骑士；过来，费边；让我们悄悄地讲几句聪明话。

薇 奥 拉　　他说起西巴斯辛的名字，
　　　　　　我哥哥正是我镜中影子，
　　　　　　兄妹俩生就一般的形状，
　　　　　　再加上穿扮得一模一样；
　　　　　　但愿暴风雨真发了慈心，
　　　　　　无情的波浪变作了多情！

　　　　　　　　　　　　下。

托　　比　　好一个刁滑的卑劣的孩子，比兔子还胆怯！他坐视朋友危急而不
　　　　　　顾，还要装作不认识，可见他刁恶的一斑，至于他的胆怯呢，问
　　　　　　费边好了。

FABIAN	A coward, a most devout coward, religious in it.
SIR ANDREW	'Slid, I'll after him again and beat him.
SIR TOBY	Do; cuff him soundly, but never draw thy sword.
SIR ANDREW	An I do not,—
FABIAN	Come, let's see the event.
SIR TOBY	I dare lay any money 'twill be nothing yet.

Exeunt.

费　　边	一个懦夫，一个把怯懦当神灵一样敬奉的懦夫。
安 德 鲁	他妈的，我要追上去把他揍一顿。
托　　比	好，把他狠狠地揍一顿，可是别拔出你的剑来。
安 德 鲁	要是我不——
费　　边	来，让我们去瞧去。
托　　比	我可以赌无论多少钱，到头来不会有什么事发生的。

　　　　　　同下。

ACT IV 第四幕

SCENE I

Before OLIVIA's house.
Enter SEBASTIAN and Clown.

Clown Will you make me believe that I am not sent for you?

SEBASTIAN Go to, go to, thou art a foolish fellow:
Let me be clear of thee.

Clown Well held out, i' faith! No, I do not know you; nor I am not sent to you by my lady, to bid you come speak with her; nor your name is not Master Cesario; nor this is not my nose neither. Nothing that is so is so.

SEBASTIAN I prithee, vent thy folly somewhere else: Thou know'st not me.

Clown Vent my folly! he has heard that word of some great man and now applies it to a fool. Vent my folly! I am afraid this great lubber, the world, will prove a cockney. I prithee now, ungird thy strangeness and tell me what I shall vent to my lady: shall I vent to her that thou art coming?

SEBASTIAN I prithee, foolish Greek, depart from me: There's money for thee: if you tarry longer, I shall give worse payment.

Clown By my troth, thou hast an open hand. These wise men that give fools money get themselves a good report after fourteen years' purchase.

Enter SIR ANDREW, SIR TOBY BELCH, and FABIAN.

SIR ANDREW Now, sir, have I met you again? there's for you.

SEBASTIAN Why, there's for thee, and there, and there. Are all the people mad?

SIR TOBY Hold, sir, or I'll throw your dagger o'er the house.

Clown This will I tell my lady straight: I would not be in some of your coats for two pence.

第一场

奥丽维娅宅旁街道。
西巴斯辛及小丑上。

小　　丑　　你要我相信我不是差来请你的吗？

西巴斯辛　　算了吧，算了吧，你是个傻瓜；给我走开去。

小　　丑　　装腔装得真好！是的，我不认识你；我的小姐也不会差我来请你去讲话；你的名字也不是西萨里奥大爷。什么都不是。

西巴斯辛　　请你到别处去大放厥词吧，你又不认识我。

小　　丑　　大放厥词！他从什么大人物那儿听了这句话，却来用在一个傻瓜身上。大放厥词！我担心整个痴愚的世界都要装腔作态起来了。请你别那么怯生生的，告诉我应当向我的小姐放些什么"厥词"。要不要对她说你就来？

西巴斯辛　　傻东西，请你走开吧。这儿有钱给你，要是你再不去，我可就要不客气了。

小　　丑　　真的，你倒是很慷慨。这种聪明人把钱给傻子，就像用十四年的收益来买一句好话。

安德鲁上。托比及费边上。

安 德 鲁　　呀，朋友，我又碰见你了吗？吃这一下。（击西巴斯辛）

西巴斯辛　　怎么，给你尝尝这一下，这一下，这一下！（打安德鲁）所有的人们都疯了吗？

托　　比　　停住，朋友，否则我要把你的刀子摔到屋子里去了。

小　　丑　　我就去把这事告诉我的小姐。我不愿凭两便士就代人受过。

Exit.

SIR TOBY Come on, sir; hold.

SIR ANDREW Nay, let him alone: I'll go another way to work with him; I'll have an action of battery against him, if there be any law in Illyria: though I struck him first, yet it's no matter for that.

SEBASTIAN Let go thy hand.

SIR TOBY Come, sir, I will not let you go. Come, my young soldier, put up your iron: you are well fleshed; come on.

SEBASTIAN I will be free from thee. What wouldst thou now? If thou dar'st tempt me further, draw thy sword.

SIR TOBY What, what? Nay, then I must have an ounce or two of this malapert blood from you.

Enter OLIVIA.

OLIVIA Hold, Toby; on thy life I charge thee, hold!

SIR TOBY Madam!

OLIVIA Will it be ever thus? Ungracious wretch,
Fit for the mountains and the barbarous caves,
Where manners ne'er were preach'd! out of my sight!
Be not offended, dear Cesario.
Rudesby, be gone!

Exeunt SIR TOBY BELCH, SIR ANDREW, and FABIAN.

I prithee, gentle friend,
Let thy fair wisdom, not thy passion, sway
In this uncivil and thou unjust extent
Against thy peace. Go with me to my house,
And hear thou there how many fruitless pranks
This ruffian hath botch'd up, that thou thereby
Mayst smile at this: thou shalt not choose but go:

下。

托　　比　（拉西巴斯辛）算了，朋友，住手吧。
安 德 鲁　不，让他去吧。我要换一个法儿对付他。要是伊利里亚是有法律的话，我要告他非法殴打的罪；虽然是我先动手，可是那没有关系。
西巴斯辛　放下你的手！
托　　比　算了吧，朋友，我不能放走你。来，我的青年的勇士，放下你的家伙。你打架已经打够了，来吧。
西巴斯辛　你别想抓住我。（挣脱）现在你要怎样？要是你有胆子的话，拔出你的剑来吧。
托　　比　什么！什么！那么我倒要让你流几滴莽撞的血呢。（拔剑）

奥丽维娅上。

奥丽维娅　住手，托比！我命令你！
托　　比　小姐！
奥丽维娅　有这等事吗？忘恩的恶人！只配住在从来不懂得礼貌的山林和洞窟里的。滚开！——别生气，亲爱的西萨里奥。——莽汉，走开！

托比、安德鲁、费边同下。

好朋友，你是个有见识的人，这回的惊扰实在太失礼、太不成话了，请你不要生气。跟我到舍下去吧，我可以告诉你这个恶人曾经多少次无缘无故地惹是招非，你听了就可以把这回事情一笑置之了。你一定要去的。
别推托！他灵魂该受天戳，
为你惊起了我心头小鹿。

第十二夜

	Do not deny. Beshrew his soul for me,
	He started one poor heart of mine in thee.
SEBASTIAN	What relish is in this? how runs the stream?
	Or I am mad, or else this is a dream:
	Let fancy still my sense in Lethe steep;
	If it be thus to dream, still let me sleep!
OLIVIA	Nay, come, I prithee; would thou'dst be ruled by me!
SEBASTIAN	Madam, I will.
OLIVIA	O, say so, and so be!

Exeunt.

西巴斯辛	滋味难名，不识其中奥妙；
	是疯眼昏迷？是梦魂颠倒？
	愿心魂永远在忘河沉浸；
	有这般好梦再不需梦醒！
丽维娅	请你来吧，你得听我的话。
西巴斯辛	小姐，遵命。
奥丽维娅	但愿这回非假！

　　　　　同下。

SCENE II

A room in OLIVIA's house.
Enter MARIA and Clown, MALVOLIO Holding a black gown.

MARIA	Nay, I prithee, put on this gown and this beard; make him believe thou art Sir Topas the curate: do it quickly; I'll call Sir Toby the whilst.

Exit.

Clown	Well, I'll put it on, and I will dissemble myself in't; and I would I were the first that ever dissembled in such a gown. I am not tall enough to become the function well, nor lean enough to be thought a good student; but to be said an honest man and a good housekeeper goes as fairly as to say a careful man and a great scholar. The competitors enter.

Enter SIR TOBY BELCH and MARIA.

SIR TOBY	Jove bless thee, master Parson.
Clown	Bonos dies, Sir Toby: for, as the old hermit of Prague, that never saw pen and ink, very wittily said to a niece of King Gorboduc, 'That that is is;' so I, being Master Parson, am Master Parson; for, what is 'that' but 'that,' and 'is' but 'is'?
SIR TOBY	To him, Sir Topas.
Clown	What, ho, I say! peace in this prison!
SIR TOBY	The knave counterfeits well; a good knave.
MALVOLIO	*[Within]* Who calls there?
Clown	Sir Topas the curate, who comes to visit
MALVOLIO	the lunatic. Sir Topas, Sir Topas, good Sir Topas, go to my lady.
Clown	Out, hyperbolical fiend! how vexest thou this man! Talkest thou nothing but of ladies?

第二场

奥丽维娅宅中一室。

玛利娅及小丑上；马伏里奥在相接的暗室内。

玛利娅　　哦，我请你把这件袍子穿上，这把胡须套上，让他相信你是副牧师托巴斯师傅。快些，我就去叫托比老爷来。

下。

小　丑　　好，我就穿起来，假装一下。我希望我是第一个扮作这种样子的。我的身材不够高，穿起来不怎么神气，略为胖一点，也不像个用功念书的。可是给人称赞一声是个老实汉子和很好的当家人，也就跟一个用心思的读书人一样好了。——那两个同党的来了。

托比·培尔契爵士及玛利娅上。

托　比　　上帝祝福你，牧师先生！

小　丑　　早安，托比大人！目不识丁的布拉格的老隐士曾经向高波杜克王的侄女说过这么一句聪明话："是什么，就是什么。"因此，我既是牧师先生，也就是牧师先生；因为"什么"即是"什么"，"是"即是"是"。

托　比　　走过去，托巴斯师傅。

小　丑　　呃哼，喂！这监狱里平安呀！

托　比　　这小子装得很像，好小子。

马伏里奥　（在内）谁在叫？

小　丑　　副牧师托巴斯师傅来看疯人马伏里奥来了。

马伏里奥　托巴斯师傅，托巴斯师傅，托巴斯好师傅，请您到我小姐那儿去一趟。

小　丑　　滚你的，胡言乱道的魔鬼！瞧这个人给你缠得这样子！只晓得嚷小姐吗？

SIR TOBY	Well said, Master Parson.
MALVOLIO	Sir Topas, never was man thus wronged: good Sir Topas, do not think I am mad: they have laid me here in hideous darkness.
Clown	Fie, thou dishonest Satan! I call thee by the most modest terms; for I am one of those gentle ones that will use the devil himself with courtesy: sayest thou that house is dark?
MALVOLIO	As hell, Sir Topas.
Clown	Why it hath bay windows transparent as barricadoes, and the clerestories toward the south-north are as lustrous as ebony; and yet complainest thou of obstruction?
MALVOLIO	I am not mad, Sir Topas: I say to you, this house is dark.
Clown	Madman, thou errest: I say, there is no darkness but ignorance; in which thou art more puzzled than the Egyptians in their fog.
MALVOLIO	I say, this house is as dark as ignorance, though ignorance were as dark as hell; and I say, there was never man thus abused. I am no more mad than you are: make the trial of it in any constant question.
Clown	What is the opinion of Pythagoras concerning wild fowl?
MALVOLIO	That the soul of our grandam might haply inhabit a bird.
Clown	What thinkest thou of his opinion?
MALVOLIO	I think nobly of the soul, and no way approve his opinion.
Clown	Fare thee well. Remain thou still in darkness: thou shalt hold the opinion of Pythagoras ere I will allow of thy wits, and fear to kill a woodcock, lest thou dispossess the soul of thy grandam. Fare thee well.
MALVOLIO	Sir Topas, Sir Topas!
SIR TOBY	My most exquisite Sir Topas!
Clown	Nay, I am for all waters.
MARIA	Thou mightst have done this without thy beard and gown: he sees thee not.

| 托 比 | 说得好,牧师先生。 |
| 马伏里奥 | (在内)托巴斯师傅,从来不曾有人给人这样冤枉过。托巴斯好师傅,别以为我疯了。他们把我关在这个暗无天日的地方。 |

| 小 丑 | 啐,你这不老实的撒旦!我用最客气的称呼叫你,因为我是个最有礼貌的人,即使对于魔鬼也不肯失礼。你说这屋子是黑的吗? |

| 马伏里奥 | 像地狱一样,托巴斯师傅。 |
| 小 丑 | 嘿,它的凸窗像壁垒一样透明,它的向着南北方的顶窗像乌木一样发光呢。你还说看不见吗? |

马伏里奥	我没有发疯,托巴斯师傅。我对您说,这屋子是黑的。
小 丑	疯子,你错了。我对你说,世间并无黑暗,只有愚昧。埃及人在大雾中辨不清方向,还不及你在愚昧里那样发昏。
马伏里奥	我说,这座屋子简直像愚昧一样黑暗,即使愚昧是像地狱一样黑暗。我说,从来不曾有人给人这样欺侮过。我并不比您更疯;您不妨提出几个合理的问题来问我,试试我疯不疯。

小 丑	毕达哥拉斯对于野鸟有什么意见?
马伏里奥	他说我们祖母的灵魂也许曾经在鸟儿的身体里寄住过。
小 丑	你对于他的意见觉得怎样?
马伏里奥	我认为灵魂是高贵的,绝对不赞成他的说法。
小 丑	再见,你在黑暗里住下去吧。等到你赞成了毕达哥拉斯的说法之后,我才可以承认你的头脑健全。留心别打山鹬,因为也许你要害得你祖母的灵魂流离失所了。再见。

马伏里奥	托巴斯师傅!托巴斯师傅!
托 比	我的了不得的托巴斯师傅!
小 丑	嘿,我可真是多才多艺呢。
玛利娅	你就是不挂胡须不穿道袍也没有关系,他又看不见你。

SIR TOBY	To him in thine own voice, and bring me word how thou findest him: I would we were well rid of this knavery. If he may be conveniently delivered, I would he were, for I am now so far in offence with my niece that I cannot pursue with any safety this sport to the upshot. Come by and by to my chamber.

Exeunt SIR TOBY BELCH and MARIA.

Clown	*[Singing]* 'Hey, Robin, jolly Robin, Tell me how thy lady does.'
MALVOLIO	Fool!
Clown	'My lady is unkind, perdy.'
MALVOLIO	Fool!
Clown	'Alas, why is she so?'
MALVOLIO	Fool, I say!
Clown	'She loves another'—Who calls, ha?
MALVOLIO	Good fool, as ever thou wilt deserve well at my hand, help me to a candle, and pen, ink and paper: as I am a gentleman, I will live to be thankful to thee for't.
Clown	Master Malvolio?
MALVOLIO	Ay, good fool.
Clown	Alas, sir, how fell you besides your five wits?
MALVOLIO	Fool, there was never a man so notoriously abused: I am as well in my wits, fool, as thou art.
Clown	But as well? then you are mad indeed, if you be no better in your wits than a fool.
MALVOLIO	They have here propertied me; keep me in darkness, send ministers to me, asses, and do all they can to face me out of my wits.
Clown	Advise you what you say; the minister is here.

| 托 | 比 | 你再用你自己的口音去对他说话,怎样的情形再来告诉我。我希望这场恶作剧快快告个段落。要是不妨把他释放,我看就放了他吧,因为我已经大大地失去了我侄女的欢心,倘把这玩意儿尽管闹下去,恐怕不大妥当。等会儿到我的屋子里来吧。 |

托比、玛利娅下。

小	丑	(唱)
		嗨,罗宾,快活的罗宾哥,
		问你的姑娘近况如何。
马伏里奥		傻子!
小	丑	不骗你,她心肠有点硬。
马伏里奥		傻子!
小	丑	唉,为了什么原因,请问?
马伏里奥		喂,傻子!
小	丑	她已经爱上了别人。——嘿!谁叫我?
马伏里奥		好傻子,谢谢你给我拿一支蜡烛、笔、墨水和纸张来,以后我不会亏待你的。君子不扯谎,我永远感你的恩。

小	丑	马伏里奥大爷吗?
马伏里奥		是的,好傻子。
小	丑	唉,大爷,您怎么会发起疯来呢?
马伏里奥		傻子,从来不曾有人给人这样欺侮过。我的头脑跟你一样清楚呢,傻子。
小	丑	跟我一样?那么您真的是疯了,要是您的头脑跟傻子差不多。
马伏里奥		他们把我当作一件家具看待,把我关在黑暗里,差牧师们——那些蠢驴子!——来看我,千方百计想把我弄昏了头。
小	丑	您说话留点神吧,牧师就在这儿呢。——马伏里奥,马伏里奥,

	Malvolio, Malvolio, thy wits the heavens restore! endeavour thyself to sleep, and leave thy vain bibble-babble.
MALVOLIO	Sir Topas!
Clown	Maintain no words with him, good fellow. Who, I, sir? not I, sir. God be wi' you, good Sir Topas. Merry, amen. I will, sir, I will.
MALVOLIO	Fool, fool, fool, I say!
Clown	Alas, sir, be patient. What say you sir? I am shent for speaking to you.
MALVOLIO	Good fool, help me to some light and some paper: I tell thee, I am as well in my wits as any man in Illyria.
Clown	Well-a-day that you were, sir
MALVOLIO	By this hand, I am. Good fool, some ink, paper and light; and convey what I will set down to my lady: it shall advantage thee more than ever the bearing of letter did.
Clown	I will help you to't. But tell me true, are you not mad indeed? or do you but counterfeit?
MALVOLIO	Believe me, I am not; I tell thee true.
Clown	Nay, I'll ne'er believe a madman till I see his brains. I will fetch you light and paper and ink.
MALVOLIO	Fool, I'll requite it in the highest degree: I prithee, be gone.
Clown	*[Singing]* I am gone, sir, And anon, sir, I'll be with you again, In a trice, Like to the old Vice, Your need to sustain; Who, with dagger of lath, In his rage and his wrath, Cries, ah, ha! to the devil:

上天保佑你明白过来吧！好好地睡睡觉儿，别啰哩啰唆地讲空话。

马伏里奥 托巴斯师傅！

小　　丑 别跟他说话，好伙计。——谁？我吗，师傅？我可不要跟他说话哩，师傅。上帝和您同在，好托巴斯师傅！——呃，阿门！——好的，师傅，好的。

马伏里奥 傻子，傻子，傻子，我对你说！

小　　丑 唉，大爷，您耐心吧！您怎么说，师傅？——师傅怪我跟您说话哩。

马伏里奥 好傻子，给我拿一点儿灯火和纸张来。我对你说，我跟伊利里亚无论哪个人一样头脑清楚呢。

小　　丑 唉，我巴不得这样呢，大爷！

马伏里奥 我可以举手发誓我没有发疯。好傻子，拿墨水、纸和灯火来，我写好之后，你去替我送给小姐。你送了这封信去，一定会到手一笔空前的大赏赐的。

小　　丑 我愿意帮您的忙。但是老实告诉我，您是不是真的疯了，还是装疯？

马伏里奥 相信我，我没有发疯，我老实告诉你。

小　　丑 嘿，我可信不过一个疯子的话，除非我能看见他的脑子。我去给您拿蜡烛、纸和墨水。

马伏里奥 傻子，我一定会重重报答你。请你去吧。

小　　丑 （唱）

大爷我去了，

请您不要吵，

不多一会的时光，

小鬼再来见魔王；

手拿木板刀，

胸中如火烧，

向着魔鬼打哈哈，

样子像个疯娃娃：

爹爹不要恼，

Like a mad lad,
Pare thy nails, dad;
Adieu, good man devil.

Exit.

给您剪指甲,
　再见,我的魔王爷!

　　　　　　　下。

SCENE III

OLIVIA's garden.
Enter SEBASTIAN.

SEBASTIAN This is the air; that is the glorious sun;
This pearl she gave me, I do feel't and see't;
And though 'tis wonder that enwraps me thus,
Yet 'tis not madness. Where's Antonio, then?
I could not find him at the Elephant:
Yet there he was; and there I found this credit,
That he did range the town to seek me out.
His counsel now might do me golden service;
For though my soul disputes well with my sense,
That this may be some error, but no madness,
Yet doth this accident and flood of fortune
So far exceed all instance, all discourse,
That I am ready to distrust mine eyes
And wrangle with my reason that persuades me
To any other trust but that I am mad
Or else the lady's mad; yet, if 'twere so,
She could not sway her house, command her followers,
Take and give back affairs and their dispatch
With such a smooth, discreet and stable bearing
As I perceive she does: there's something in't
That is deceiveable. But here the lady comes.

Enter OLIVIA and Priest.

OLIVIA Blame not this haste of mine. If you mean well,
Now go with me and with this holy man
Into the chantry by: there, before him,
And underneath that consecrated roof,

第三场

奥丽维娅的花园。
西巴斯辛上。

西巴斯辛 这是空气；那是灿烂的太阳；这是她给我的珍珠，我看得见也摸得到。虽然怪事这样包围着我，然而却不是疯狂。那么安东尼奥到哪儿去了呢？我在大象旅店里找不到他，可是他曾经到过那边，据说他到城中各处寻找我去了。现在我很需要他的指教；因为虽然我心里很觉得这也许是出于错误，而并非是一种疯狂的举动，可是这种意外和飞来的好运太有些未之前闻，无可理解了，我简直不敢相信我的眼睛。无论我的理智怎样向我解释，我总觉得不是我疯了便是这位小姐疯了。可是，真是这样的话，她一定不会那样井井有条，神气那么端庄地操持她的家务，指挥她的仆人，料理一切的事情，如同我所看见的那样。其中一定有些蹊跷。她来了。

奥丽维娅及一牧师上。

奥丽维娅 不要怪我太性急。要是你没有坏心肠的话，现在就跟我和这位神父到我家的礼拜堂里去吧；当着他的面前，在那座圣堂的屋顶下，你要向我充分证明你的忠诚，好让我小气的、多疑的心安定下来。他可以保守秘密，直到你愿意宣布出来按照着我的身份的

                Plight me the full assurance of your faith;
                That my most jealous and too doubtful soul
                May live at peace. He shall conceal it
                Whiles you are willing it shall come to note,
                What time we will our celebration keep
                According to my birth. What do you say?
SEBASTIAN I'll follow this good man, and go with you;
                And, having sworn truth, ever will be true.
OLIVIA   Then lead the way, good father; and heavens so shine,
                That they may fairly note this act of mine!

Exeunt.

婚礼将在那时候举行。你说怎样？

西巴斯辛　我愿意跟你们两位前往；
　　　　　立过的盟誓永没有欺罔。
奥丽维娅　走吧，神父，但愿天公作美，
　　　　　一片阳光照着我们酣醉！

　　　　　　　　　同下。

ACT V 第五幕

SCENE I

A street before OLIVIA's house.
Enter Clown and FABIAN.

FABIAN	Now, as thou lovest me, let me see his letter.
Clown	Good Master Fabian, grant me another request.
FABIAN	Any thing.
Clown	Do not desire to see this letter.
FABIAN	This is, to give a dog, and in recompense desire my dog again.

Enter DUKE ORSINO, VIOLA, CURIO, and Lords.

DUKE	Belong you to the Lady Olivia, friends?
Clown	Ay, sir; we are some of her trappings.
DUKE	I know thee well; how dost thou, my good fellow?
Clown	Truly, sir, the better for my foes and the worse for my friends.
DUKE	Just the contrary; the better for thy friends.
Clown	No, sir, the worse.
DUKE	How can that be?
Clown	Marry, sir, they praise me and make an ass of me; now my foes tell me plainly I am an ass: so that by my foes, sir I profit in the knowledge of myself, and by my friends, I am abused: so that, conclusions to be as kisses, if your four negatives make your two affirmatives why then, the worse for my friends and the better for my foes.
DUKE	Why, this is excellent.
Clown	By my troth, sir, no; though it please you to be one of my friends.
DUKE	Thou shalt not be the worse for me: there's gold.
Clown	But that it would be double-dealing, sir, I would you could make it another.

第一场

奥丽维娅宅前街道。
小丑及费边上。

费　边　看在咱们交情的分上,让我瞧一瞧他的信吧。
小　丑　好费边先生,允许我一个请求。
费　边　尽管说吧。
小　丑　别向我要这封信看。
费　边　这就是说,把一条狗给了人,要求的代价是,再把那条狗要还。

公爵、薇奥拉、丘里奥及侍从等上。

公　爵　朋友们,你们是奥丽维娅小姐府中的人吗?
小　丑　是的,殿下,我们是附属于她的一两件零星小物。
公　爵　我认识你。你好吗,我的好朋友?
小　丑　不瞒您说,殿下,我的仇敌使我好些,我的朋友使我坏些。
公　爵　恰恰相反,你的朋友使你好些。
小　丑　不,殿下,坏些。
公　爵　为什么呢?
小　丑　呃,殿下,他们称赞我,把我当作驴子一样愚弄。可是我的仇敌却坦白地告诉我说我是一头驴子。因此,殿下,多亏我的仇敌我才能明白我自己,我的朋友却把我欺骗了。因此,结论就像接吻一样,说四声"不"就等于说两声"请",这样一来,当然是朋友使我坏些,仇敌使我好些了。

公　爵　啊,这说得好极了!
小　丑　凭良心说,殿下,这一点不好,虽然您愿意做我的朋友。

公　爵　我不会使你坏些。这儿是钱。
小　丑　倘不是恐怕犯了骗人钱财的罪名,殿下,我倒希望您把它再加一倍。

DUKE	O, you give me ill counsel.
Clown	Put your grace in your pocket, sir, for this once, and let your flesh and blood obey it.
DUKE	Well, I will be so much a sinner, to be a double dealer: there's another.
Clown	Primo, secundo, tertio, is a good play; and the old saying is, the third pays for all: the triplex, sir, is a good tripping measure; or the bells of Saint Bennet, sir, may put you in mind; one, two, three.
DUKE	You can fool no more money out of me at this throw: if you will let your lady know I am here to speak with her, and bring her along with you, it may awake my bounty further.
Clown	Marry, sir, lullaby to your bounty till I come again. I go, sir; but I would not have you to think that my desire of having is the sin of covetousness: but, as you say, sir, let your bounty take a nap, I will awake it anon.

Exit.

VIOLA	Here comes the man, sir, that did rescue me.

Enter ANTONIO and Officers.

DUKE	That face of his I do remember well; Yet, when I saw it last, it was besmear'd As black as Vulcan in the smoke of war: A bawbling vessel was he captain of, For shallow draught and bulk unprizable; With which such scathful grapple did he make With the most noble bottom of our fleet, That very envy and the tongue of loss Cried fame and honour on him. What's the matter?

公　　爵　啊，你给我出的好主意。

小　　丑　把您的慷慨的手伸进您的袋里去，殿下，只这一次，不要犹疑吧。

公　　爵　好吧，我姑且来一次罪上加罪，拿去。

小　　丑　掷骰子有幺二三；古话说，"一不做，二不休，三回才算数"；跳舞要用三拍子；您只要听圣班纳特教堂的钟声好了，殿下——一，二，三。

公　　爵　你这回可骗不动我的钱了。要是你愿意去对你小姐说我在这儿要见她说话，同着她到这儿来，那么也许会再唤醒我的慷慨来的。

小　　丑　好吧，殿下，给您的慷慨唱个安眠歌，等着我回来吧。我去了，殿下。可是我希望您明白我要钱并不是贪财。好吧，殿下，就照您的话，让您的慷慨打个盹儿，我等一会儿再来叫醒他吧。

下。

薇奥拉　殿下，这儿来的人就是搭救了我的。

安东尼奥及警吏上。

公　　爵　他那张脸我记得很清楚。可是上次我见他的时候，他脸上涂得黑黑的，就像烽烟里的乌尔冈一样。他是一只吃水量和体积都很小的舰上的舰长，可是却使我们舰队中最好的船只大遭损失，就是心怀嫉恨的、给他打败的人也不得不佩服他。为了什么事？

First Officer Orsino, this is that Antonio that took the Phoenix and her
Fraught from Candy;
And this is he that did the Tiger board,
When your young nephew Titus lost his leg:
Here in the streets, desperate of shame and state,
In private brabble did we apprehend him.

VIOLA He did me kindness, sir, drew on my side;
But in conclusion put strange speech upon me:
I know not what 'twas but distraction.

DUKE Notable pirate! thou salt-water thief!
What foolish boldness brought thee to their mercies,
Whom thou, in terms so bloody and so dear,
Hast made thine enemies?

ANTONIO Orsino, noble sir,
Be pleased that I shake off these names you give me:
Antonio never yet was thief or pirate,
Though I confess, on base and ground enough,
Orsino's enemy. A witchcraft drew me hither:
That most ingrateful boy there by your side,
From the rude sea's enraged and foamy mouth
Did I redeem; a wreck past hope he was:
His life I gave him and did thereto add
My love, without retention or restraint,
All his in dedication; for his sake
Did I expose myself, pure for his love,
Into the danger of this adverse town;
Drew to defend him when he was beset:
Where being apprehended, his false cunning,
Not meaning to partake with me in danger,
Taught him to face me out of his acquaintance,
And grew a twenty years removed thing

警吏	启禀殿下,这就是在坎迪地方把"凤凰号"和它的货物劫了去的安东尼奥;也就是在"猛虎号"上把您的侄公子泰特斯削去了腿的那人。我们在这儿的街道上看见他穷极无赖,在跟人家打架,因此抓了来了。
薇奥拉	殿下,他曾经拔刀相助,帮过我忙,可是后来却对我说了一番奇怪的话,似乎发了疯似的。
公　爵	好一个海盗!在水上行窃的贼徒!你怎么敢凭着你的愚勇,投身到被你用血肉和巨量的代价结下冤仇的人们的手里呢?
安东尼奥	尊贵的奥西诺,请许我洗刷去您给我的称呼。安东尼奥从来不曾做过海盗或贼徒,虽然我有充分的理由和原因承认我是奥西诺的敌人。一种魔法把我吸引到这儿来。在您身边的那个最没有良心的孩子,是我从汹涌的怒海的吞噬中救了出来的,否则他已经毫无希望了。我给了他生命,又把我的友情无条件地完全给了他;为了他的缘故,纯粹出于爱心,我冒着危险出现在这个敌对的城里,见他给人包围了,就拔剑相助。可是我遭了逮捕,他的狡恶的心肠因恐我连累他受罪,便假装不认识我,一霎眼就像已经暌违了二十年似的,甚至于我在半点钟前给他任意使用的我自己的钱袋,也不肯还给我。

	While one would wink; denied me mine own purse,

                  While one would wink; denied me mine own purse,
                  Which I had recommended to his use
                  Not half an hour before.

VIOLA   How can this be?

DUKE   When came he to this town?

ANTONIO   To-day, my lord; and for three months before,
                  No interim, not a minute's vacancy,
                  Both day and night did we keep company.

                  Enter OLIVIA and Attendants.

DUKE   Here comes the countess: now heaven walks on earth.
                  But for thee, fellow; fellow, thy words are madness:
                  Three months this youth hath tended upon me;
                  But more of that anon. Take him aside.

OLIVIA   What would my lord, but that he may not have,
                  Wherein Olivia may seem serviceable?
                  Cesario, you do not keep promise with me.

VIOLA   Madam!

DUKE   Gracious Olivia,—

OLIVIA   What do you say, Cesario? Good my lord,—

VIOLA   My lord would speak; my duty hushes me.

OLIVIA   If it be aught to the old tune, my lord,
                  It is as fat and fulsome to mine ear
                  As howling after music.

DUKE   Still so cruel?

OLIVIA   Still so constant, lord.

DUKE   What, to perverseness? you uncivil lady,
                  To whose ingrate and unauspicio us altars
                  My soul the faithfull'st offerings hath breathed out
                  That e'er devotion tender'd! What shall I do?

OLIVIA   Even what it please my lord, that shall become him.

薇奥拉	怎么会有这种事呢?
公　爵	他在什么时候到这城里来的?
安东尼奥	今天,殿下,三个月来,我们朝朝夜夜都在一起,不曾有一分钟分离过。

奥丽维娅及侍从等上。

公　爵	这里来的是伯爵小姐,天神降临人世了!——可是你这家伙,完全在说疯话;这孩子已经待候我三个月了。那种话等会儿再说吧,把他带到一旁去。
奥丽维娅	殿下有什么下示?除了断难遵命的一件事之外,凡是奥丽维娅力量所能及的,一定愿意效劳。——西萨里奥,你失了我的约啦。
薇奥拉	小姐!
公　爵	温柔的奥丽维娅!——
奥丽维娅	你怎么说,西萨里奥?——殿下——
薇奥拉	我的主人要跟您说话,因为地位关系我不能开口。
奥丽维娅	殿下,要是您说的仍旧是那么一套,我可已经听厌了,就像奏过音乐以后的叫号一样令人不耐。
公　爵	仍旧是那么残酷吗?
奥丽维娅	仍旧是那么坚定,殿下。
公　爵	什么,坚定得不肯改变一下你的乖僻吗?你这无礼的女郎!向着你的无情的不仁的祭坛,我的灵魂已经用无比的虔诚吐露出最忠心的献礼。我还有什么办法呢?
奥丽维娅	办法就请殿下自己斟酌吧。

DUKE	Why should I not, had I the heart to do it,
	Like to the Egyptian thief at point of death,
	Kill what I love?—a savage jealousy
	That sometimes savours nobly. But hear me this:
	Since you to non-regardance cast my faith,
	And that I partly know the instrument
	That screws me from my true place in your favour,
	Live you the marble-breasted tyrant still;
	But this your minion, whom I know you love,
	And whom, by heaven I swear, I tender dearly,
	Him will I tear out of that cruel eye,
	Where he sits crowned in his master's spite.
	Come, boy, with me; my thoughts are ripe in mischief:
	I'll sacrifice the lamb that I do love,
	To spite a raven's heart within a dove.
VIOLA	And I, most jocund, apt and willingly,
	To do you rest, a thousand deaths would die.
OLIVIA	Where goes Cesario?
VIOLA	After him I love
	More than I love these eyes, more than my life,
	More, by all mores, than e'er I shall love wife.
	If I do feign, you witnesses above
	Punish my life for tainting of my love!
OLIVIA	Ay me, detested! how am I beguiled!
VIOLA	Who does beguile you? who does do you wrong?
OLIVIA	Hast thou forgot thyself? is it so long?
	Call forth the holy father.*(Exit an Attendant)*
DUKE	*[to OLIVIA]*Come, away!
OLIVIA	Whither, my lord? Cesario, husband, stay.
DUKE	Husband!
OLIVIA	Ay, husband: can he that deny?

| 公　　爵 | 假如我狠得起那么一条心，为什么我不可以像临死时的埃及大盗[①]一样，把我所爱的人杀死了呢？蛮性的嫉妒有时也带着几分高贵的气质。但是你听着我说：既然你漠视我的诚意，我也有些知道谁在你的心中夺去了我的位置，你就继续做你的铁石心肠的暴君吧；可是你所爱着的这个宝贝，我当天发誓我曾经那样宠爱着他，我要把他从你的那双冷酷的眼睛里除去，免得他傲视他的主人。来，孩子，跟我来。我的恶念已经成熟： |

我要牺牲我钟爱的羔羊，
白鸽的外貌乌鸦的心肠。（走）

薇奥拉	我甘心愿受一千次死罪，
	只要您的心里得到安慰。（随行）
奥丽维娅	西萨里奥到哪儿去？
薇奥拉	追随我所爱的人，
	我爱他甚于生命和眼睛，
	远过于对于妻子的爱情。
	愿上天鉴察我一片诚挚，
	倘有虚谎我决不辞一死！
奥丽维娅	哎哟，他厌弃了我！我受了欺骗了！
薇奥拉	谁把你欺骗？谁给你受气？
奥丽维娅	才不久你难道已经忘记？——请神父来。（一侍从下）
公　　爵	（向薇奥拉）去吧！
奥丽维娅	到哪里去，殿下？西萨里奥，我的夫，别去！
公　　爵	你的夫？

① 事见赫利俄多洛斯(Heliodorus)所著希腊浪漫故事《埃塞俄比亚人》(Ethiopica)。

DUKE	Her husband, sirrah!
VIOLA	No, my lord, not I.
OLIVIA	Alas, it is the baseness of thy fear
	That makes thee strangle thy propriety:
	Fear not, Cesario; take thy fortunes up;
	Be that thou know'st thou art, and then thou art
	As great as that thou fear'st.

Enter Priest.

OLIVIA	O, welcome, father!
	Father, I charge thee, by thy reverence,
	Here to unfold, though lately we intended
	To keep in darkness what occasion now
	Reveals before 'tis ripe, what thou dost know
	Hath newly pass'd between this youth and me.
Priest	A contract of eternal bond of love,
	Confirm'd by mutual joinder of your hands,
	Attested by the holy close of lips,
	Strengthen'd by interchangement of your rings;
	And all the ceremony of this compact
	Seal'd in my function, by my testimony:
	Since when, my watch hath told me, toward my grave
	I have travell'd but two hours.
DUKE	O thou dissembling cub! what wilt thou be
	When time hath sow'd a grizzle on thy case?
	Or will not else thy craft so quickly grow,
	That thine own trip shall be thine overthrow?
	Farewell, and take her; but direct thy feet
	Where thou and I henceforth may never meet.
VIOLA	My lord, I do protest—
OLIVIA	O, do not swear!

奥丽维娅　　是的,我的夫。他能抵赖吗?
公　　爵　　她的夫,嘿?
薇奥拉　　不,殿下,我不是。
奥丽维娅　　唉!是你的卑怯的恐惧使你否认了自己的身份。不要害怕,西萨里奥,别放弃了你的地位。你知道你是什么人,要是承认了出来,你就跟你所害怕的人并肩相埒了。

　　　　　　　　　　　牧师上。

奥丽维娅　　啊,欢迎,神父!神父,我请你凭着你的可尊敬的身份,到这里来宣布你所知道的关于这位少年和我之间不久以前的事情;虽然我们本来预备保守秘密,但现在不得不在时机未到之前公布了。

牧　　师　　一个永久相爱的盟约,已经由你们两人握手缔结,用神圣的吻证明,用戒指的交换确定了。这婚约的一切仪式,都由我主持作证;照我的表上所指示,距离现在我不过向我的坟墓走了两小时的行程。

公　　爵　　唉,你这骗人的小畜生!等你年纪一大了起来,你会是个怎样的人呢?
　　　　　　也许你过分早熟的奸诡,
　　　　　　反会害你自己身败名毁。
　　　　　　别了,你尽管和她论嫁娶;
　　　　　　可留心以后别和我相遇。
薇奥拉　　殿下,我要声明——
奥丽维娅　　不要发誓;

Hold little faith, though thou hast too much fear.

Enter SIR ANDREW AGUECHEEK with his head broken.

SIR ANDREW	For the love of God, a surgeon! Send one presently to Sir Toby.
OLIVIA	What's the matter?
SIR ANDREW	He has broke my head across and has given Sir Toby a bloody coxcomb too: for the love of God, your help! I had rather than forty pound I were at home.
OLIVIA	Who has done this, Sir Andrew?
SIR ANDREW	The count's gentleman, one Cesario: we took him for a coward, but he's the very devil incardinate.
DUKE	My gentleman, Cesario?
SIR ANDREW	'Od's lifelings, here he is! You broke my head for nothing; and that that I did, I was set on to do't by Sir Toby.
VIOLA	Why do you speak to me? I never hurt you: You drew your sword upon me without cause; But I bespoke you fair, and hurt you not.
SIR ANDREW	If a bloody coxcomb be a hurt, you have hurt me: I think you set nothing by a bloody coxcomb.

Enter SIR TOBY BELCH and Clown.

	Here comes Sir Toby halting; you shall hear more: but if he had not been in drink, he would have tickled you othergates than he did.
DUKE	How now, gentleman! how is't with you?
SIR TOBY	That's all one: has hurt me, and there's the end on't. Sot, didst see Dick surgeon, sot?
Clown	O, he's drunk, Sir Toby, an hour agone; his eyes were set at eight i' the morning.

放大胆些，别亵渎了神祇！

安德鲁·艾古契克爵士头破血流上。

安 德 鲁	看在上帝的分上，叫个外科医生来吧！立刻去请一个来瞧瞧托比爵士。
奥丽维娅	什么事？
安 德 鲁	他把我的头给打破了，托比爵士也给他弄得满头是血。看在上帝的分上，救救命吧！谁要是给我四十镑钱，我也宁愿回到家里去。
奥丽维娅	谁干了这种事，安德鲁爵士？
安 德 鲁	公爵的跟班名叫西萨里奥的。我们把他当作一个孱头，哪晓得他简直是个魔鬼。
公 爵	我的跟班西萨里奥？
安 德 鲁	他妈的！他就在这儿。你无缘无故敲破我的头！我不过是给托比爵士怂恿了才动手的。
薇奥拉	你为什么对我说这种话呢？我没有伤害你呀。你自己无缘无故向我拔剑；可是我对你很客气，并没有伤害你。
安 德 鲁	假如一颗血淋淋的头可以算得是伤害的话，你已经把我伤害了；我想你以为满头是血，是算不了一回事的。托比爵士一跷一拐地来了——

托比·培尔契爵士由小丑搀扶醉步上。

你等着瞧吧，如果他刚才不是喝醉了，你一定会尝到他的厉害手段。

公 爵	怎么，老兄！你怎么啦？
托 比	有什么关系？他把我打坏了，还有什么别的说的？傻瓜，你有没有看见狄克医生，傻瓜？
小 丑	喔！他在一个钟头之前喝醉了，托比老爷，他的眼睛在早上八点钟就昏花了。

SIR TOBY	Then he's a rogue, and a passymeasures pavin: I hate a drunken rogue.
OLIVIA	Away with him! Who hath made this havoc with them?
SIR ANDREW	I'll help you, Sir Toby, because we'll be dressed together.
SIR TOBY	Will you help? an ass-head and a coxcomb and a knave, a thin-faced knave, a gull!
OLIVIA	Get him to bed, and let his hurt be look'd to.

Exeunt Clown, FABIAN, SIR TOBY BELCH, and SIR ANDREW.
Enter SEBASTIAN.

SEBASTIAN	I am sorry, madam, I have hurt your kinsman: But, had it been the brother of my blood, I must have done no less with wit and safety. You throw a strange regard upon me, and by that I do perceive it hath offended you: Pardon me, sweet one, even for the vows We made each other but so late ago.
DUKE	One face, one voice, one habit, and two persons, A natural perspective, that is and is not!
SEBASTIAN	Antonio, O my dear Antonio! How have the hours rack'd and tortured me, Since I have lost thee!
ANTONIO	Sebastian are you?
SEBASTIAN	Fear'st thou that, Antonio?
ANTONIO	How have you made division of yourself? An apple, cleft in two, is not more twin Than these two creatures. Which is Sebastian?
OLIVIA	Most wonderful!
SEBASTIAN	Do I stand there? I never had a brother; Nor can there be that deity in my nature, Of here and every where. I had a sister,

| 托　　比 | 那么他便是个踱着八字步的混蛋。我顶讨厌酒鬼。 |

奥丽维娅	把他带走！谁把他们弄成这样子的？
安 德 鲁	我来扶着您吧，托比爵士，咱们一块儿裹伤口去。
托　　比	你来扶着我？蠢驴，傻瓜，混蛋，瘦脸的混蛋，笨鹅！

| 奥丽维娅 | 招呼他上床去，好好看顾一下他的伤口。 |

小丑、费边、托比、安德鲁同下。
西巴斯辛上。

| 西巴斯辛 | 小姐，我很抱歉伤了令亲。可是即使他是我的同胞兄弟，为了自卫起见我也只好出此手段。您用那样冷淡的眼光瞧着我，我知道我一定冒犯了您了；原谅我吧，好人，看在不久以前我们彼此立下的盟誓分上。 |

| 公　　爵 | 一样的面孔，一样的声音，一样的装束，化成了两个身体；一副天然的幻镜，真实和虚妄的对照！ |
| 西巴斯辛 | 安东尼奥！啊，我的亲爱的安东尼奥！自从我不见了你之后，我的时间过得多么痛苦啊！ |

安东尼奥	你是西巴斯辛吗？
西巴斯辛	难道你不相信是我吗，安东尼奥？
安东尼奥	你怎么会分身呢？把一只苹果切成两半，也不会比这两人更为相像。哪一个是西巴斯辛？

| 奥丽维娅 | 真奇怪呀！ |
| 西巴斯辛 | 那边站着的是我吗？我从来不曾有过一个兄弟；我又不是一尊无所不在的神明。我只有一个妹妹，但已经被盲目的波涛卷去了。对不住，请问你我之间有什么关系？你是哪一国人？叫什么名 |

第十二夜

	Whom the blind waves and surges have devour'd.
	Of charity, what kin are you to me?
	What countryman? what name? what parentage?
VIOLA	Of Messaline: Sebastian was my father;
	Such a Sebastian was my brother too,
	So went he suited to his watery tomb:
	If spirits can assume both form and suit
	You come to fright us.
SEBASTIAN	A spirit I am indeed;
	But am in that dimension grossly clad
	Which from the womb I did participate.
	Were you a woman, as the rest goes even,
	I should my tears let fall upon your cheek,
	And say 'Thrice-welcome, drowned Viola!'
VIOLA	My father had a mole upon his brow.
SEBASTIAN	And so had mine.
VIOLA	And died that day when Viola from her birth
	Had number'd thirteen years.
SEBASTIAN	O, that record is lively in my soul!
	He finished indeed his mortal act
	That day that made my sister thirteen years.
VIOLA	If nothing lets to make us happy both
	But this my masculine usurp'd attire,
	Do not embrace me till each circumstance
	Of place, time, fortune, do cohere and jump
	That I am Viola: which to confirm,
	I'll bring you to a captain in this town,
	Where lie my maiden weeds; by whose gentle help
	I was preserved to serve this noble count.
	All the occurrence of my fortune since
	Hath been between this lady and this lord.

字？谁是你的父母？

薇奥拉　　　我是梅萨林人。西巴斯辛是我的父亲；我的哥哥也是一个像你一样的西巴斯辛，他葬身于海洋中的时候也穿着像你一样的衣服。要是灵魂能够照着在生时的形状和服饰出现，那么你是来吓我们的。

西巴斯辛　　我的确是一个灵魂，可是还没有脱离我的生而具有的物质的皮囊。你的一切都能符合，只要你是个女人，我一定会让我的眼泪滴在你的脸上，而说，"大大地欢迎，溺死了的薇奥拉！"

薇奥拉　　　我的父亲额角上有一颗黑痣。
西巴斯辛　　我的父亲也有。
薇奥拉　　　他死的时候薇奥拉才十三岁。

西巴斯辛　　唉！那记忆还鲜明地留在我的灵魂里。他的确在我妹妹刚满十三岁的时候完毕了他人世的任务。

薇奥拉　　　假如只是我这一身僭妄的男装阻碍了我们彼此的欢欣，那么等一切关于地点、时间、遭遇的枝节完全衔接，证明我确是薇奥拉之后，再拥抱我吧。我可以叫一个在这城中的船长来为我证明，我的女衣便是寄放在他那里的；多亏他的帮忙，我才侥幸保全了生命，能够来侍候这位尊贵的公爵。此后我便一直奔走于这位小姐和这位贵人之间。

SEBASTIAN *[To OLIVIA]*
So comes it, lady, you have been mistook:
But nature to her bias drew in that.
You would have been contracted to a maid;
Nor are you therein, by my life, deceived,
You are betroth'd both to a maid and man.

DUKE Be not amazed; right noble is his blood.
If this be so, as yet the glass seems true,
I shall have share in this most happy wreck.
[To OLIVIA]
Boy, thou hast said to me a thousand times
Thou never shouldst love woman like to me.

VIOLA And all those sayings will I over-swear;
And those swearings keep as true in soul
As doth that orbed continent the fire
That severs day from night.

DUKE Give me thy hand;
And let me see thee in thy woman's weeds.

VIOLA The captain that did bring me first on shore
Hath my maid's garments: he upon some action
Is now in durance, at Malvolio's suit,
A gentleman, and follower of my lady's.

OLIVIA He shall enlarge him: fetch Malvolio hither:
And yet, alas, now I remember me,
They say, poor gentleman, he's much distract.
A most extracting frenzy of mine own
From my remembrance clearly banish'd his.

Re-enter Clown with a letter, and FABIAN.

How does he, sirrah?

Clown Truly, madam, he holds Belzebub at the staves's end as well as

西巴斯辛　　（向奥丽维娅）

小姐，原来您是弄错了，但那也是心理上的自然的倾向。您本来要跟一个女孩子订婚，可是拿我的生命起誓，您的希望并没有落空。您现在同时是一个女人和一个男人的未婚妻了。

公　　爵　　不要惊骇，他的血统也很高贵。要是这回事情果然是真，看来似乎不是一面骗人的镜子，那么在这番最幸运的覆舟里我也要沾点儿光。

（向薇奥拉）

孩子，你曾经向我说过一千次决不会像爱我一样爱着一个女人。

薇奥拉　　那一切的话我愿意再发誓证明；那一切的誓我都要坚守在心中，就像分隔昼夜的天球中蕴藏着的烈火一样。

公　　爵　　把你的手给我，让我瞧你穿了女人的衣服是什么样子。

薇奥拉　　把我带上岸来的船长那里存放着我的女服，可是他现在跟这儿小姐府上的管家马伏里奥有点讼事，被拘留起来了。

奥丽维娅　　一定要他把他放出来。去叫马伏里奥来。——唉。我现在记起来了，他们说，可怜的人，他的神经病很厉害呢。因为我自己在大发其疯，所以把他的疯病完全忘记了。

　　　　　　　　　　小丑持信及费边上。

他怎样啦，小子？

小　　丑　　启禀小姐，他总算很尽力抵挡着魔鬼。他写了一封信给您。我本

	a man in his case may do: has here writ a letter to you; I should have given't you to-day morning, but as a madman's epistles are no gospels, so it skills not much when they are delivered.
OLIVIA	Open't, and read it.
Clown	Look then to be well edified when the fool delivers the madman. *[Reads]* 'By the Lord, madam,'—
OLIVIA	How now! art thou mad?
Clown	No, madam, I do but read madness: an your ladyship will have it as it ought to be, you must allow vox.
OLIVIA	Prithee, read i' thy right wits.
Clown	So I do, madonna; but to read his right wits is to read thus: therefore perpend, my princess, and give ear.
OLIVIA	*[To FABIAN]* Read it you, sirrah.
FABIAN	*[Reads]* 'By the Lord, madam, you wrong me, and the world shall know it: though you have put me into darkness and given your drunken cousin rule over me, yet have I the benefit of my senses as well as your ladyship. I have your own letter that induced me to the semblance I put on; with the which I doubt not but to do myself much right, or you much shame. Think of me as you please. I leave my duty a little unthought of and speak out of my injury.

THE MADLY-USED MALVOLIO.

OLIVIA	Did he write this?
Clown	Ay, madam.
DUKE	This savours not much of distraction.
OLIVIA	See him deliver'd, Fabian; bring him hither.

Exit FABIAN.

My lord so please you, these things further thought on,

该今天早上就给您的，可是疯人的信不比福音，送没送到都没甚关系。

奥丽维娅　拆开来读给我听。

小　　丑　傻子要念疯子的话了，请你们洗耳恭听。（读）"凭着上帝的名义，小姐——"

奥丽维娅　怎么！你疯了吗？

小　　丑　不，小姐，我在读疯话呢。您小姐既然要我读这种东西，那么您就得准许我疯声疯气地读。

奥丽维娅　请你读得清楚一些。

小　　丑　我正是在这样做，小姐，可是他的话怎么清楚，我就只能怎么读。所以，我的好公主，请您还是全神贯注，留意倾听吧。

奥丽维娅　（向费边）喂，还是你读吧。

费　　边　（读）"凭着上帝的名义，小姐，您屈待了我；全世界都要知道这回事。虽然您已经把我幽闭在黑暗里，叫您的醉酒的令叔看管我，可是我的头脑跟您小姐一样清楚呢。您自己骗我打扮成那个样子，您的信还在我手里；我很可以用它来证明我自己的无辜，可是您的脸上却不好看哩。随您把我怎么看待吧。因为冤枉难明，不得不暂时僭越了奴仆的身份，请您原谅。"

被虐待的马伏里奥上。

奥丽维娅　这封信是他写的吗？

小　　丑　是的，小姐。

公　　爵　这倒不像是个疯子的话哩。

奥丽维娅　去把他放出来，费边；带他到这儿来。

费边下。

殿下，等您把这一切再好好考虑一下之后，如果您不嫌弃，肯认

	To think me as well a sister as a wife,
	One day shall crown the alliance on't, so please you,
	Here at my house and at my proper cost.
DUKE	Madam, I am most apt to embrace your offer.
	[To OLIVIA] Your master quits you; and
	for your service done him,
	So much against the mettle of your sex,
	So far beneath your soft and tender breeding,
	And since you call'd me master for so long,
	Here is my hand: you shall from this time be
	Your master's mistress.
OLIVIA	A sister! you are she.

Re-enter FABIAN, with MALVOLIO.

DUKE	Is this the madman?
OLIVIA	Ay, my lord, this same.
	How now, Malvolio!
MALVOLIO	Madam, you have done me wrong,
	Notorious wrong.
OLIVIA	Have I, Malvolio? no.
MALVOLIO	Lady, you have. Pray you, peruse that letter.
	You must not now deny it is your hand:
	Write from it, if you can, in hand or phrase;
	Or say 'tis not your seal, nor your invention:
	You can say none of this: well, grant it then
	And tell me, in the modesty of honour,
	Why you have given me such clear lights of favour,
	Bade me come smiling and cross-garter'd to you,
	To put on yellow stockings and to frown
	Upon Sir Toby and the lighter people;
	And, acting this in an obedient hope,

	我做一个亲戚，而不是妻子，那么同一天将庆祝我们两家的婚礼，地点就在我家，费用也由我来承担。
公　　爵	小姐，多蒙厚意，敢不领情。（向薇奥拉）你的主人解除了你的职务了。你事主多么勤劳，全然不顾那种职务多么不适于你的娇弱的身份和优雅的教养；你既然一直把我称作主人，从此以后，你便是你主人的主妇了。握着我的手吧。
奥丽维娅	你是我的妹妹了！

费边偕马伏里奥重上。

公　　爵	这便是那个疯子吗？
奥丽维娅	是的，殿下，就是他。——怎样，马伏里奥！
马伏里奥	小姐，您屈待了我，大大地屈待了我！
奥丽维娅	我屈待了你吗，马伏里奥？没有的事。
马伏里奥	小姐，您屈待了我。请您瞧这封信。您能抵赖说那不是您写的吗？您能写几笔跟这不同的字，几句跟这不同的句子吗？您能说这不是您的图章，不是您的大作吗？您可不能否认。好，那么承认了吧；凭着您的贞洁告诉我：为什么您向我表示这种露骨的恩意，吩咐我见您的时候脸带笑容，扎着十字交叉的袜带，穿着黄袜子，对托比大人和底下人要皱眉头？我满心怀着希望，一切服从您，您怎么要把我关起来，禁锢在暗室里，叫牧师来看我，给人当作闻所未闻的大傻瓜愚弄？告诉我为什么？

	Why have you suffer'd me to be imprison'd,

                    Why have you suffer'd me to be imprison'd,
                    Kept in a dark house, visited by the priest,
                    And made the most notorious geck and gull
                    That e'er invention play'd on? tell me why.

OLIVIA   Alas, Malvolio, this is not my writing,
                    Though, I confess, much like the character
                    But out of question 'tis Maria's hand.
                    And now I do bethink me, it was she
                    First told me thou wast mad; then cam'st in smiling,
                    And in such forms which here were presupposed
                    Upon thee in the letter. Prithee, be content:
                    This practise hath most shrewdly pass'd upon thee;
                    But when we know the grounds and authors of it,
                    Thou shalt be both the plaintiff and the judge
                    Of thine own cause.

FABIAN   Good madam, hear me speak,
                    And let no quarrel nor no brawl to come
                    Taint the condition of this present hour,
                    Which I have wonder'd at. In hope it shall not,
                    Most freely I confess, myself and Toby
                    Set this device against Malvolio here,
                    Upon some stubborn and uncourteous parts
                    We had conceived against him: Maria writ
                    The letter at Sir Toby's great importance;
                    In recompense whereof he hath married her.
                    How with a sportful malice it was follow'd,
                    May rather pluck on laughter than revenge;
                    If that the injuries be justly weigh'd
                    That have on both sides pass'd.

OLIVIA   Alas, poor fool, how have they baffled thee!

Clown   Why, 'some are born great, some achieve greatness, and

奥丽维娅 唉！马伏里奥，这不是我写的，虽然我承认很像我的笔迹，但这一定是玛利娅写的。现在我记起来了，第一个告诉我你发疯了的就是她，那时你便一路带笑而来，打扮和动作的样子就跟信里所说的一样。你别恼吧，这场诡计未免太恶作剧，等我们调查明白原因和主谋的人之后，你可以自己兼作原告和审判官来判断这件案子。

费　边 好小姐，听我说，不要让争闹和口角来打断了当前这个使我惊喜交加地好时光。我希望您不会见怪，我坦白地承认是我跟托比老爷因为看不上眼这个马伏里奥的顽固无礼，才想出这个计策来。因为托比老爷央求不过，玛利娅才写了这封信。为了酬劳她，他已经跟她结了婚了。假如把两方所受到的难堪衡情酌理地判断起来，那么这种恶作剧的戏谑可供一笑，也不必计较了吧。

奥丽维娅 唉，可怜的傻子，他们太把你欺侮了！

小　丑 嘿，"有的人是生来的富贵，有的人是挣来的富贵，有的人是送

some have greatness thrown upon them.' I was one, sir, in this interlude; one Sir Topas, sir; but that's all one. 'By the Lord, fool, I am not mad.'

But do you remember? 'Madam, why laugh you at such a barren rascal? an you smile not, he's gagged:' and thus the whirligig of time brings in his revenges.

MALVOLIO I'll be revenged on the whole pack of you.

Exit.

OLIVIA He hath been most notoriously abused.
DUKE Pursue him and entreat him to a peace:
He hath not told us of the captain yet:
When that is known and golden time convents,
A solemn combination shall be made
Of our dear souls. Meantime, sweet sister,
We will not part from hence. Cesario, come;
For so you shall be, while you are a man;
But when in other habits you are seen,
Orsino's mistress and his fancy's queen.

Exeunt all, except Clown.

Clown *[Sings]*
When that I was and a little tiny boy,
With hey, ho, the wind and the rain,
A foolish thing was but a toy,
For the rain it raineth every day.
But when I came to man's estate,
With hey, ho,
'Gainst knaves and thieves men shut their gate,
For the rain,

上来的富贵。"这本戏文里我也是一个角色呢，大爷，托巴斯师傅就是我，大爷；但这没有什么相干。"凭着上帝起誓，傻子，我没有疯。"可是您记得吗？"小姐，您为什么要对这么一个没头脑的混蛋发笑？您要是不笑，他就开不了口啦。"六十年风水轮流转，您也遭了报应了。

马伏里奥　我一定要出这一口气，你们这批东西一个都不放过。

下。

奥丽维娅　他给人欺侮得太不成话了。

公　　爵　追他回来，跟他讲个和。他还不曾把那船长的事告诉我们哩；等我们知道了以后，假如时辰吉利，我们便可以举行郑重的结合的典礼。贤妹，我们现在还不会离开这儿。西萨里奥，来吧，当你还是一个男人的时候，你便是西萨里奥——等你换过了别样的衣裙，
你才是奥西诺心上情人。

除小丑外均下。

小　　丑　（唱）
　　　　　当初我是个小儿郎，
　　　　　　嗨，呵，一阵雨儿一阵风；
　　　　　做了傻事毫不思量，
　　　　　　朝朝雨雨呀又风风。
　　　　　年纪长大啦不学好，
　　　　　　嗨，呵，一阵雨儿一阵风；
　　　　　闭门羹到处吃个饱，
　　　　　　朝朝雨雨呀又风风。

But when I came, alas! to wive,
With hey, ho,
By swaggering could I never thrive,
For the rain,
But when I came unto my beds,
With hey, ho,
With toss-pots still had drunken heads,
For the rain,
A great while ago the world begun,
With hey, ho,
But that's all one, our play is done,
And we'll strive to please you every day.

Exit.

娶了老婆,唉!要照顾,
嗨,呵,一阵雨儿一阵风;
法螺医不了肚子饿,
朝朝雨雨呀又风风。
一壶老酒往头里灌,
嗨,呵,一阵雨儿一阵风;
掀开了被窝三不管,
朝朝雨雨呀又风风。
开天辟地有几多年,
嗨,呵,一阵雨儿一阵风;
咱们的戏文早完篇,
愿诸君欢喜笑融融!

　　　　　下。